The Sovei

Will Hickey

The Sovereignty Game

Neo-Colonialism and the Westphalian System

Will Hickey
Former two-time US Fulbright
Professor, 2003 & 2009
Professor of Management, GDUFS
Canton, China

ISBN 978-981-15-1890-4   ISBN 978-981-15-1888-1   (eBook)
https://doi.org/10.1007/978-981-15-1888-1

Cover image: © Kanchisa Thitisukthanapong

This Palgrave Macmillan imprint is published by the registered company Springer Nature
Singapore Pte Ltd.
The registered company address is: 152 Beach Road, #21-01/04 Gateway East, Singapore
189721, Singapore

Prologue

The world we live in is now vastly overpopulated with significant "public goods" problems affecting the whole of humanity. Simply, if you pump enough CO_2 into the atmosphere, the world will overheat; if you dump enough plastic rubbish in the seas, it will filter up the food chain; if you allow enough foreign migrants to cross your borders, it will change your country's cultural and socioeconomic balances.

The Westphalian denominator of the nation-state is considered infallible and unquestionable, but 350 years ago, this framework did not exist. It was a solution to problems then that has become in itself, a problem of today. Westphalia can co-opt, as colonial powers in the twentieth century did, (Sykes–Picot) and in itself be co-opted as we are seeing with emerging China (South China Sea islets and salami-slicing).

Fighting the world's fires in a Westphalian system is essentially restricting mankind to fighting with one hand tied behind his back. Westphalia, similar to the *Magna Carta* in 1215, is about protecting the special interests and entitlements of those with much to lose. It was never about concerns for the everyman. We simply don't live in that kind of landed world anymore with our information overload, AI, telecommunications, digitalization and data analytics. In the modern era of self-actualization, why should anyone be a prisoner to a boundary, an ideology, a passport, or arbitrary decision of an unelected (or even elected) leader? Where is the empowerment? Maybe we need to consider the system then, as the ultimate foundation problem, and not the symptoms that arise from it.

The Westphalian denominator is extremely powerful. It has decided wars, underpinned religion, promoted economic growth, and has given major causation to otherwise, nonevents. It will not be easy to overcome this defaulted thinking. Consider the Football World Cup or the Olympics. Nation pitted against nation in a seemingly "life or death" struggle on a pitch, a track, or a swimming pool. Many of these nations themselves ascripted of people groups so ethnically and culturally diverse it seemingly defies the original intent of Westphalia: like-minded and culturally socioeconomic groups.

A step back shows however that Westphalia today is more a prognosticator of problems than a creator of shared solutions. Climate change thus becomes a political football, as do many other public goods problems such as immigration and plastic trash that will never be neatly solved under a framework of exclusivity. Treaties and conventions only go as far as the willpower of the subscribers, or the weakest nation-state that supports it.

This book is not merely some semantical political theory or a fun history lesson down memory lane. It is a call to recognition and action that the old system rooted in the seventeenth-century political world simply cannot deliver in the twenty-first century of interconnectedness across borders and is poisonous. It is not beyond the writer to realize that people will cling to a bad system and the elites that support it, if no other system is offered. Westphalia is so ingrained and understood as statist in our world that it is beyond scrutiny. Or is it? Our planet simply cannot afford blind abeyance anymore for old constructs to deliver remedies. The stakes have never been higher and mankind's survival, not just living standards, depends on serious changes. The world needs a governance system that fits the twenty-first century and beyond, not one from the seventeenth century. Whether this will be demonstrated in world of political convergence or divergence is still unknown.

Bali   Dr. Will Hickey
January 2020

CONTENTS

LIST OF FIGURES

CHAPTER 1

Dismantling the Westphalian System in Today's "Age of Reason"

PRETEXT

The Peace of Westphalia was a conference arranged between the warring entities of France, Hapsburg Germany, Sweden, Denmark, Dutch Spain, and Holy Roman principalities in the Spring of 1648. They were fighting over political and religious disagreement between Catholics, Swiss Calvinists, and Protestants, with the fall of the Holy Roman Empire, that had manifested in the Protestant Reformation that was countered by the Catholic inquisitions. In short, it was a very messy time of religious conflict and chaos. Elites in charge sought stability.

The Peace culminated in the signing of treaties of Munster in May 1648, and later in Osnabruck, in October 1648, in what is now modern Germany by the many imperial and religious delegations sent on behalf of the kingdoms and various entities that they represented. The Venetians served as mediators.[1] The treaties ended the Thirty Years' War (1618–1648) and the religious conflict between the Papacy and Lutheranism (though not all hostilities ceased), and set in motion a new system of sovereign nations and boundaries with non-interference in others affairs as a right of exclusivity. Switzerland was recognized as an independent country, as was Holland, from Spain. The kingdom of Sweden in the north, and France in the west, divided considerable territory between them and what is now modern-day Germany. Religion was given as equal (secular) before

© The Author(s) 2020
W. Hickey, *The Sovereignty Game*,
https://doi.org/10.1007/978-981-15-1888-1_1

the law, with territorial rulers allowed to determine which was legally recognized. A new political start to years of religious and territorial chaos. Of course not all agreed, with the Holy See and Papacy considering the settlement as deeply unjust.

The decline of the Holy Roman Empire and end of the Thirty Years' War were long and complicated political-religious events that have convoluted histories. This book does not discuss that historical narrative, though these issues deeply affected the motivations and thinking at that time, but rather what political manifestation the substance of The Peace of Westphalia has led us to now. The Peace of Westphalia was about the power to bring this new ideal of regional exclusivity to differing ideas, cultures, and religions, in the then-nouveau concept of the "nation-state", or the creation of the international system. That ideal, while criticized in the past,[2] is now being put to the test today. Simply, a single claim of universal rule may now be necessary to return to what was left off in 1648 and restarted in this twenty-first century, namely, one definitive authority to set order amongst uncertainty, however politically unpalatable that may be to some, or perhaps to even revisit the highly contentious issue of "one-world governance". George Soros theme of *reflexivity*, (reality at first distanced then converged with a cognition or awareness) to create a new paradigm reinforced from previous events, comes to mind. Which, and according to Henry Kissinger, was what the world was pushing toward *before* Westphalia (due to endless wars fueled by religion and imperialism), but not one participant (religious, dynastic, or imperial) had the individual might or political alliances in place to push this construct forward post-Reformation. Only *pyrrhic* victories were being had in both blood and treasure. It was the alarmed and empowered elites in these nations who called for changes, to put an end to cycles of continuously vicious wars, for their own self-survival and wealth preservation.

But what really is the nation, according to Hegel, Marx, Kissinger, and North? Not merely in their theories, but also in their deeds. Today, humanity faces similar threats, not so much from religious wars, but from public goods issues: climate change, plastic garbage, uncontrollable economic migration, etc. Can empowered elites deliver this time? A key question is where precisely does the power of the sovereign state evolve from?

We consider Westphalian viewpoints from three perspectives, economic, philosophic, and historical. The debate about the current world order, namely, the denominator of the nation-state, is structured around the entire concept of Westphalia.

Westphalia is based on exclusivity, which is all but dead in today's interconnected, digital world

INTRODUCTION

If one looks at the world from space, no national borders can be seen, at all, anywhere. The view is of a geographical expanse of continents, fertile areas, deserts, seas, oceans, valleys, mountains, and islands all with their own natural boundaries and demarcations. That is the natural order of things. However, when one is on the ground, it is a different reality. Man-made borders and limits exist, on land, in the sea, and in the air. Some borders are visible, some not. Breaching these borders willfully, without permission, will usually result in severe consequences and punishment. This is the order of a man-made system, known as the Peace of Westphalia, that was perfected 350 years ago in a conference to end ongoing European continental wars fueled mostly by religious and dynastic disagreement, in an area of northern Germany. It set the pretext for the formation of the modern "nation-state" which today we assume as a normal and un-debated reference point.

The Westphalian system of nation-states then (herein defined as simply, "Westphalia") is the post-reformation construct of sovereign state governance that still exists as the foundation for all modern countries today. It enshrined three exclusivity principles in the treaty for the formation of the modern nation-state: (1) State sovereignty, (2) Equality of the state, and (3) Non-interference in the internal affairs of one state to another. The third point is the most critical and relevant to pressing global issues today, in particular in an overpopulated world that is consistently diverging politically. Westphalia is simply rooted in a very different historical narrative and understanding of the world as we now know it.

A precursor to Westphalia was the *Magna Carta*, or "Great Charter" of 1215, when a group of English nobles demanded legal and property rights from the English King, John I. The *Divine Rights of Kings* was until then, the codified rule of the land. What the king controlled, he ruled and was the unquestioned judge, jury, and executioner of all his subjects. Like the Magna Carta, it was the elites and people at the top ("nobles") who benefit the most from the Westphalian construct, and still do to this day. These concepts are not new. Throughout history, all societies, be they feudal, communist, dynastic, animist, or democratic: elites have emerged to rule, guide, and be served by those in the rest of the masses of society. Equanimity nor egalitarianism has never been a hallmark of mankind's systems of governance, no matter how much effort was expended on democracy as an enlightened form of perfected governance given. Westphalia is not an inalienable concept in itself, yet is presented that way as to certify elite interests and to gain buy-in from the other "Two Estates". Westphalia is simply an ordering system demanded in times of great political, religious, and cultural chaos.

Concepts of "national borders" were not well developed up until the Peace of Westphalia. Walls, such as Hadrian's Wall, built by the Roman Empire in Britain, and the Great Wall, built by the Chinese, usually marked the administrative boundaries of any given empire against hostile, non-defined, frontiers. During Frankish times, steps were taken to demarcate borders in what is now central Europe and Italy, by creating baronies and duchies. At the apex of the high Middle ages, and with ongoing Crusades to the Middle East that brought back the rich spoils of conquest, provincial barons and dukes were beginning to garner wealth, territory, and military power for themselves that they did not want to share with far off regents or in particular, the Papacy, which was the originator of the crusades in 1095.

Without consensus and support from these said barons and religious leaders, kings could not wage war and claim distant lands. Consensus dictated compromise. The Magna Carta, despite any contemporary grade school historic interpretations to the contrary, never had anything to do with the rights of the common Medieval man: be he peasant or serf. It was about elites serving and protecting the interests of other elites, a "self-reinforcement" of their system, with its strength found in unity and numbers.

When Thomas Jefferson penned the US Declaration of Independence 550 years later, in summer 1776, and 56 previously British colonial subjects signed it, the definition of "citizens" also had a narrow connotation: White, Protestant, adult male, property owners, over 21, in essence the "elite strata" of that day. In that privileged sense, the Declaration of Independence was similar in design to the Magna Carta: that being to fit a very targeted audience, protecting their wealth and power.

The Thirty Years' War and Germanic Movements as a Foundation for Westphalia

Westphalia was a product of the Reformation. But especially important inasmuch of the ultimate result of the Reformation is the struggle of the Protestant church for a political existence, in particular in Germany. The Protestant Church, even as it occurred directly, interfered frequently in secular affairs causing worldly entanglements and disputes over political possessions. Subjects of Catholic princes became Protestant, and claimed rights to church property, altering the nature of these possessions.

In Germany conditions were still advantageous to Protestantism, in that the special former imperial fiefs had now become principalities. But in countries like Austria, the Protestants stood partly without the princes, partly against them, and in France they had to be given fortresses for the safety of their religious practices. Without wars, the existence of Protestantism would never have been secured, because it was not their conscience, but the political and private possessions, which were seized against the rights of the church and were later reclaimed by them. This constant fighting and chaos between Protestants and Catholics was essentially at the core of the Thirty Years' War, and led to Westphalia.

Through the **Peace of Westphalia** the Protestant church was then recognized as independent, bringing tremendous humiliation to the Catholic church. This peace has often been thought of as the German palladium because it established a political constitution for Germany. But in fact this constitution was **a declaration of the private rights of the countries into which it had fallen. There was no thought to and no idea on the *purpose* of a state**.

In Westphalia there is expressed the purpose of perfect particularity, and the private law determines the exclusivity of all relations; and that all relations are so determined by private law so that the interests of the individual parts to act for themselves against the interest of the whole, or to refrain from doing what their interest demands and or even **required by law**, is kept and secured in a most inviolable manner. In other words, the state reigns supreme and settles legal issues exclusively within its own borders.

Immediately after the Westphalian declaration **it became clear that the German Reich was a state against others**: it led to further ignominious wars against the Turks, from which Vienna had to be liberated by the Poles. Even more questionable was its relationship with France, which during the peace took possession of free cities, the defensive walls of Germany, and prosperous provinces and, without effort, kept them.

Hegel on the Peace of Westphalia: People, Wars, and Religion

In order to understand Westphalia more clearly from a Germanic philosophical level, one should also contemplate more deeply what the nation-state meant then, in the mid-seventeenth century, versus what it means now, and ask if the paradigm shift really matters? We consider then the writings of nineteenth-century German philosopher G. W. F. Hegel, (1770–1831) who held the concept of the state in high esteem and commented extensively on Westphalia.[3] The state, in Hegel's view, was near God in design, concept, and purposes. In Hegel's ideal world, people don't exist as isolated atoms, but as members of a political community.[4] The state gives them a form and meaning to this community. It is not determined by ethnicity or religion (not any particular religion that is) or by skin or race, etc. We can see that Hegel was the first philosopher to idealize what the state really was, and additionally, had the necessary national framework to consider it. From Hegel in Werkes,

> *The health of a state is generally not revealed so much in the quiet of peace as in the movement of war; the former is the state of enjoyment and activity in isolation, the government a wise patriarchy that demands only ordinary things for the ruled; but in war, the power of the connection of all with the whole shows how much it has been able to demand of them, and how much that is good, what from their own instinct and their heart they may do for it.*

The result of the struggle, then, were the religious factions, constrained by force and now politically motivated, existing side by side as political states according to positive state or private law relations. **But further and later, the Protestant Church completed its political guarantee that one of its member states be elevated to an independent European power**. This power, Prussia, reemerged with Protestantism which, occurred at the end of the seventeenth century.

Above are all from *Werke I*, Early writings, The German Constitution, pp. 451–610 [written by Hegel 1800–1802].

Thus, through the political community (which needs a state, a government of some kind to give it shape, form, and spatiality) one can attain a reality that goes beyond one's own individual self. So the political community is, in a way, the realization of the individual. The individual becomes that embodiment. We consider Hegel's quote from his Lectures on the Philosophy of History (translated),[5] about the Thirty Years' War:

> *Thus, in the war with the French Republic, Germany experienced no longer being a state, and it has become politically conditioned, both in the war itself and in the peace that ended this war and whose tangible results are: Loss of some of the most beautiful German lands, of some millions of its inhabitants, a debt burden in the southern half more than on the northern, which extends the misery of war far into peace, and that except those which come under the rule of the conquerors and at the same time foreign laws and customs have come, many more states will lose what is their highest good - actually being states*

and

> *All the powers of Europe, with few exceptions, now plunge into Germany, whither they flow back as to the source from which they had emanated, and where now the right of current religious intimacy and the right of inner separateness shall be fought. The struggle ends without idea, without having gained a principle as thought, with the fatigue of all, the complete devastation in which all forces had been shattered, and the mere letting happen and existence of the of the sides on the basis of external power. The outcome is only political.*

The takeaway here is that Hegel sees the outcome, including the peace agreement, of the Thirty Years' War as having no substantial principle or idea as a result. The next quote is the most explicit statement by Hegel on the Peace of Westphalia.

> *Wars, whether they are called wars of aggression or of defiance - about which designation the parties never agree - would be called unfair only if the peace agreements stipulated unconditional reciprocal peace; and if the expression of eternal peace and eternal friendship between the powers also has this expression, then it is to be understood as the limitation in the nature of the matter: before any part is attacked or treated with hostility. No state can be bound to be treated with hostility or attacked and yet not to defend themselves, but to keep peace.*

Hegel thus takes a negative long-term view of the peace agreement as it regards Germany's constitution, because it solidified the independence of the German states at the cost of the German empire (*das Deutsche*

Reich). Hegel grounds this on the then-current thought, in the minds of Germans, as to what a real German freedom would be, that being in terms of the German Reich. The freedom of the independent German princedoms is detrimental to the other freedom. Frequently Hegel refers to these two competing notions of freedom (the sense of political freedom of the state, rather than the individuals freedom). The law itself preserves this splintered notion of the state. Also, in relation to other states, the agreement was to Germany's disadvantage.

In the German constitution, Hegel's text of 1800–1801, there are many references to the Westphalian Peace, but not with a clear positive statement of Hegel's view of it in terms of European history, but rather mostly in terms of its negative results for Germany, which had to wait another fifty years to see in Prussia someone come to the fore as a leader of Germany (Otto von Bismarck). Germany was only really united as a country with Bismark in the second half of the nineteenth century (well after Hegel was deceased) and not by any declaration at Westphalia in 1648.

The following long translations do not touch on the Westphalian Peace of 1648 directly, but it clearly establishes that, for Hegel, the state principle is independent of religion, language, and other features of culture (though naturally these do play some role, of course).

In our times there may be an equally loose connection or none at all among the members [of a state] *in terms of manners, education, and language; and their identity, this former cornerstone of a people's union, is now to be counted among the contingencies whose nature does not prevent a group from constituting a state power. Rome or Athens, and any modern small state, could not exist if the many languages in use in the Russian Empire were spoken within its sphere, just as little if among its citizens the customs were as different as they were in that empire or as they and the education already are in every capital of a big country. The difference between language and dialects, which at the same time makes separation even more irritating than the total incomprehensibility, the diversity of customs and education in the separate estates, which makes men almost only recognizable by their external appearance at the same time the most powerful elements are capable of overpowering and holding together in the modern states the spirit and art of the state organizations, as in the great Roman empire, so that inequality of education and customs is a necessary product and a necessary condition in modern states.*

That in religion, in that in which the innermost being of men expresses itself and, even if all other external and scattered things may be indifferent, they nevertheless recognize themselves as in a fixed center, and only thus, beyond inequality [and] variation of other relations and conditions, can trust one another and to be sure of one another - that here at least is an identity - has also been found to be dispensable in newer states.

As little before and after, in the separation into peoples, has the identity of religion prevented wars and bound them into one state, so in our times the non-identity of religion does not tear apart a state. The state power, as a pure constitutional right, has had to separate itself from religious power and its right and maintained its own existence enough that it [the state] need the church and has put it back into the state of separation it had in its origins with the Roman state.

Of course, according to the theories of the state, which in our times have been set up partly by pseudo philosophers and human rights teachers and partly realized in huge political experiments, all the rest – except the most important, language, education, morals, and religion – of what we have excluded from the necessary concept of state power, subjected to the direct activity of the highest state power, and indeed in such a way that it determines that all these sides, to their smallest threads, are attracted by it.
p. 500 [and the German states divided from each other]

The Peace of Westphalia then did not deal with the problem of the German nation-state. Nor did it in general, have anything to do with the issue of nation-states as we know them now at that time. It concerned the relationships between states (sovereign states), and said nothing at all about nation-states, this derivation evolved much later. Of course, some issues of nation or people were involved, since that had some bearing, at least, on the notion of a state, such as in the majority religion of its people, but this was purely political in nature. Better consequences came to those countries with more power, a better bargaining position. The agreements recognized state boundaries quite independent of the notion of nation. The boundaries weren't religious either, though religion is not the same as a nation. Germany itself was and still is two religions, Protestant and Catholic, each almost equally (and now today maybe a quarter atheist).

The above reflections and philosophy concerns the internal features of the state (the political unity that bonds a group of people living under its jurisdiction), and is in principle independent of any particular racial, religious, linguistic, or cultural features. For Hegel, the political is higher than all these others.

So what about the religious aspect, of which the Thirty Years' War between Protestants, Catholics, and others were fought? Hegel's theology is rooted in Protestant Christianity, but it has gone beyond historical Christianity since, and in that sense is secular (or might be considered so by deeply religious people). Hegel certainly never really indicated pure secularity. Religion is not the core or basis of the state for Hegel but considered the state as God's sanction for man on earth. Even if the Westphalian Peace settled religious boundaries (it certainly didn't) that is not what state means for Hegel, but rather just the opposite, that the state is what exists in common even when there are two or three different religions.

There are certain religious factions and cultures such as the Islamic State culture, Dynasticism, and Marxism, that are all, by their nature, incompatible with democratic institutions. But the "state as God" in reality basically means that the state does in the practical, or physical what religion does in the spiritual, or esoteric. It realizes morality, as it unifies the community, it gives people a reason to live beyond their own individual life on earth. All these ideas are consistent with Hegel's philosophy. The following quote again indicates that, for Hegel, religion (pluralistically) is not the basis for the unity of any state:

> *But when religion completely destroyed the state, it miraculously gave us the notion of some principles on which a state can rest. When splitting apart people in their innermost being there still must remain a bond, so they must bond externally regarding external things, the conduct of wars, famine, pestilence, natural disasters, etc -- a bond that is the principle of modern states. The very fact that the most important parts of constitutional law were woven into the religious division, two religions have been woven into the state and thus made all political rights dependent on two or actually three religions, it has been contravened by the principle of the independence of the state from the church and the possibility of a state, irrespective of the diversity of religions, and in fact, by the existence of different religions and by the fact that Germany is a state, it has been recognized.*

Overall, however, Hegel was negative about the outcomes of Westphalia.

> *Without going back to the old days, let us give an overview of how the Peace of Westphalia expressed Germany's impotence, its fate in relation to external powers and the extent of its territory; what Germany's loss through peace has been; for the damage caused by the war itself is immeasurable in all respect.*

Hegel then today would be skeptical of globalism, as it has manifested itself today in the nation-state context. Mainly, it is an issue of individualism. Hegel was a strong proponent of individualism and personal liberty, not just in passing, but in the core of his theory, his logic is based on the three categories of the universal, the particular, and the individual. For Hegel, the individual combines the universal and the particular. The state, the sovereign, plays into this logic. The state is universal in the sense that it embodies all citizens, and it is particular in that it is one state among others, demonstrating its own exceptionalism (however that may be defined), and the individuality is this state as a particular state embodies a universal (all citizens) and also moves forward toward higher levels of universality—i.e., women gain the vote, minorities civil rights are enforced, some may even say, demands a "universal basic income", etc.

The following is the complaint Hegel makes that the treaty of Westphalia which in essence then gave Germany the *wrong* kind of freedom.

"*The Peace of Westphalia completely consolidated the principle of what was then called German freedom, namely, the dissolution of the empire into independent states, diminished the number of such independent states, the only remaining possibility of a higher authority of the whole over the parts, and strengthened the separation through their merging into larger states, and granted foreign powers a legitimate interference in internal affairs, partly by granting them imperial lands, partly by making them guarantors of the constitution.*" But there is more that again expresses Hegel's dissatisfaction with the Westphalian Peace:

> *In the Peace of Westphalia, this statelessness of Germany became organized. Writers like Hippolytus a Lapide have certainly expressed the inner character and tendency of the nation. In the Peace of Westphalia, Germany gave up establishing itself as a secure state power, and abandoned itself to the goodwill of its members.*

The following, again, is more of Hegel's criticism of the Peace of West-phalia:

> *It is the Peace of Westphalia that has fixed this relationship of the indepen-dence of the parts. They would not have been able to do so by themselves, but rather, their bond was atomized, as were they themselves and their countries, with no possibility of their own resistance, in Ferdinand's (the King of Spain) political and religious despotism.*

And more of the same in the following:

> *In the Peace of Westphalia, the sovereignty, or at least the emperor's supremacy over imperial cities which belonged to the emperors and which belonged to the imperial cities, i.e. their magistrates, pledged in the course of time, have been declared undeliverable. The magistrate set by the emperor, or whatever title he had in other cities, always had to receive the magistrates with a certain respect. They were under the watchful eyes of a person independent of them, who had to bear some weight because of their connection with the head of the Empire. Since the imperial cities in the Peace of Westphalia were fully safeguarded by the state power pledged to them, their freedom of one sort has been fully secured, the other kind of freedom has suffered more and more...*

Again, Hegel's idea of German state (*staat*) but meaning the "Reich":

> *An existence of the German Reich would be possible only when a state power would be organized and the German people again would come into relation with Kaiser (king) and Reich (state).*

where

> *The Peace of Westphalia is one of the most important basic laws governing the possession of any state; what power is it that would sustain it and the rest of the imperial laws and peace agreements.*

> *In the Peace of Westphalia itself, all those who would be offended in respect to the rights are allowed to take possession of themselves through self-help; in order to do this, one must have enough power to do so -- the attack or self-help becomes a matter of calculation and politics.*

Hegel wrote a famous dialectic of master and slave in the early chapters of his Phenomenology of Mind, and in that context it is very clear that he understands historical and even individual development as a process of fighting for freedom, and in these process stages of servitude are traversed, and necessary to their being overcome. In other words, in Hegel's day, **the state had real meaning, to protect culture, ethnicity, and religion(s) and create and promulgate a unique, national identity.** Globalism, big data, instantaneous communications, and mass migration have certainly changed that original mandate. Culture, religion, ethnicity, are subjugated to secularism, though beliefs are rooted deeply in people's psyche from birth.

Today, nation-states, both weak and strong, have become blurred with globalism. If this is the case then, we must ask, what is the charade of a national border really representing in this era? Do monied, politically connected, and educated elites transplant the new cultures, religions, and ethnicities? Full stop: If this really is the new dynamic, then a planar modularity is being created where borders don't really matter, but rather money, skills, and political capital do. A new power paradigm begins to emerge. One that is not enshrined in a socio-cultural dynamic any longer inside specific man-made borders.

Marx Versus Hegel

A contrast to Hegel (who agrees on what the Westphalian Peace is, and yet disagrees on its importance as being a model for anything) is Karl Marx. As different as Marx is from Hegel regarding the state (Hegel considered it to be god on earth), so to speak, but nonetheless, *areligious*, Marx considered it as part of the "superstructure ideology", (in service to the ruling class). Both Hegel and Marx do agree on one thing, to understand the state, negatively or positively, the internal is just as important as the external, and in fact neither can be understood without the other, so they become two sides of one coin.

In the opening dozen or so pages of Marx's *Grundrisse*, he deals with the state in a very interesting way based on three models: France, England, and the US. The US is the most advanced political order (mainly in terms of the relation between the state and the economy), England is next, and most backward among these three on the road of development is France (Germany would be yet further behind France, if Marx had included it). He deals with two writers, the American economist Henry Carey and the French economist Frédéric Bastiat. Each has a different understanding of the role of the state, and the ideal role, due (but this unknown to them) to the stage of development of their own country. Also, whether one approves of a larger role for the state, or a smaller one, also depends on whether the sought harmony concerns international economic affairs or internal economic affairs and internal social relations. And these two, inner and outer, generally stand in opposition to one another. One is achieved at the cost of the other. Again, all this concerns economy and trade, as Nobel Laureate Douglas North also hypothesized, not war and social discord.

Of course, Marx sided with the US, for the same reason he sided with the North against the South in the Civil War, not on any moral grounds (Marx actually believed the South had the high ground when it came to morality, at least in some sense of the term), but based purely on economics in terms of historical development. The cause of the war for Marx was economic, and morally the North was bankrupt, since their motivation was purely profit and a desire to exploit workers, but in terms of historical economic development the North was definitely ahead of the South. Even slavery is condemned, using the economic criterion, not because of its inhumanity, but because of its primitiveness in terms of ultimate economic development. Marx endorsed (on grounds of economic progress) things that he morally found disgusting, such as the damage done to Indian society and economy by the British. We come to the assessment then that there is some morality in Marxism, but that is another political discourse.

Where does all this lead us then to the present situation regarding Westphalia? The idea of internal and external understanding of state and law, and the notion of state, in relation to economy, being relative to that stage of development in the economy—this means it is wrong to label Marx as either for the state or against the state. Every concrete situation will determine this, many of which Marx himself never saw. How it all equates may be debated, but there isn't a way to go into this argument with a preconceived answer—that Marx was against the state because it is a "superstructure", a word he used exactly one time in the German Ideology. Philosophically, it is much more complicated than that.

THE WESTPHALIAN SYSTEM

Westphalia then is a European, specifically Germanic, concept by derivation, born of long and various warring factions. Westphalia utilized secularism to subjugate monarchy, dynasticism (i.e., family lineage, such as in

"Han" or "Ming" China), and ethic/religious forms of governance and also largely homogenous agrarian and dynastic cultures in Africa, Asia, and South America as applied by colonial powers, with foreign mindsets and a panoply of cultural differences. The vestiges of dynasticism are still well rooted today, in these same areas, sodden with intractable and perpetual economic and political conflicts, such as in Iraq, Syria, sub-Saharan Africa, and developing South America. Namely, these are societies which are not based on the balanced, nation-state conceptual ideal, which devolved from Westphalian-style state that has come to mean those nation-states which married entire societies and leaderships to their geography and were imbued with legitimacy because of these relationships—tacit, historical, or electoral—between the societies and their governance. In short, the term Westphalian implies a sovereignty underpinned by legitimacy, and socio-cultural meaning. The term "pre-Westphalian", then, implies a form of control of a population without its consent; a lack of the rule of laws agreed to by the society, and therefore a lack sociocultural structure and order (and therefore sovereignty) as recognized by its own population.

Based on all the above logic, it is difficult to see how diversity alone can magically congeal into any "synergetic" force to confront today's cross-border direct threats to humanity, (immigration, climate change, non-state actors, extra-territoriality, immigration, and extreme economic inequality), without any overarching directive. Otherwise, sovereign governments, hiding in their Westphalian exclusivity and dystopia, will continue to default, debate, deny, bicker, obfuscate, and distort what real actions need to be taken to confront global problems in exchange for protecting what is most important to them: their self-interest and their nation-state, not global problems, which are nonetheless amplified and transmitted with instantaneous communications and media in our digital age.

Countries that embrace their sovereignty with positions of isolationism above global well-being, as with the US (for example, rejecting the Paris Accords, and not a signatory on the UN's convention on war crimes) or like China with an extreme, almost cartoonish, stand on non-interference of "internal affairs" (however broadly interpreted that may be, especially in regions such as the South China Sea, and in Tibet with very non-ethnic Chinese populations), or even Japan and Spain, with overfishing, become part of the bigger problem not the solution, and are perhaps the biggest threat to date to getting to a consensus on difficult public goods decisions.

Yet, the Westphalian system, an institution of a long bygone era, is still blindly and unquestioningly ascribed to, and threatens humanity today with its discrete, exclusive framework by failing to incorporate transnational changes on an enforceable level in order to protect and insulate elites who benefit the most from their exclusivity status quo. Regional alliances such as ASEAN, SCO, or MERCOSOR, and economic consortia, such as NAFTA, WTO, or APEC, have only superficial or one-dimensional controls over their respective member states, while Greece, Brexit and most recently, Italy (5 Star Movement) have laid bare the entrenched sovereign financial and social disconnects facing the European Union (EU) that cannot be easily dismissed, addressed, or enforced by supranational actors such as the UN, IMF, OECD, or World Bank.

POLITICAL FRAMEWORK OF WESTPHALIA

In his 2014 seminal book, '*World Order*' former Harvard History professor, then later US Secretary of State and National Security Advisor under then presidents Richard Nixon and Gerald Ford, Henry Kissinger glowingly waxes on about the history of the Peace of Westphalia in 1648 setting the stage for the world of borders and sovereignty as we know it today free from the interference of religious or imperial order. Kissinger declares it as "*the scaffolding of international order... as it now exists*" (p. 5). It was a European convent, with homogenous, white European actors: Swedes, French, Germans, Austrians and Dutch realizing that never-ending Empire building, dynastic claims, and hegemony had cost them dearly in wealth and people (indeed the Thirty Years' War was estimated to have cost Europe a quarter of its population due to combat, famine, and disease) for hundreds of years. So much barbarity existed that a generation was raised knowing anything but war. None of the antagonists could settle down and get back to what mattered to them: living without fear of want, violence, persecution, or uncertainty.

A political, not philosophical, comparison then between Henry Kissinger and Hegel may be in order here. Kissinger puts considerably more weight on states (political sovereignties of whatever form they take, some closer to nation-states, some more like the Westphalian Peace model as he takes it) in respect to their **external** relations. Whereas, Hegel's focus was more on **internal** workings. Kissinger treats the internal only somewhat in passing, as part of the picture, but not in itself determinant of the external. It should be then that Kissinger is also aware of this, and it also follows from him taking the Westphalian Peace as a standard, since it also focused on the external ideal mostly, or at least that is what Kissinger takes from it. Kissinger's tenure on the world stage ended in the 1970s it should be noted, before many public goods issues and technology advances began taking hold. Additionally, Kissinger also was a product of a 'Cold War' mentality, with mutual nuclear destruction.

Westphalia spread globally in the nineteenth century largely through imperialism. It eventually supplanted vast empires, as well as unsettled territories and cultural and ethnic areas such as in Ireland, Italy and Germany; creating an of oligopoly of governance and that claimed practically every square foot of the planet, the exceptions being the poles, whether the adherents liked it or not. The initial ideal was to have mutually recognized borders and strong international institutions to resolve conflicts and create strong neighbors. Nonetheless, the rise of political elites has created merely an illusion of political stability. Borders and territory grabs became sources of conflict for more power and resources, fueling instability.

Another tectonic shift happening in the mid-seventeenth century was that the Reformation had taken hold. Certain Northern European leaders and religious factions wanted to break the millennia-old arbitrary territorial hold and power that Rome and Catholicism had on them once and for all. In that sense, Westphalia was in fact the new secular challenge to Rome's grip on power via any papacy endorsed empire (the "king as a direct descendent of Adam", the Pope as "Gods representative on earth"), that would counter it. This was not for any deep-seated religious conviction, but rather that elites wanted to control their own identity and property, not a far away, corrupt, religion. Westphalia was used as an instrument to end religious conflict with its secularism. Ironically, Pope Frances' 2015 Encyclical on climate change, *Laudato Si*, brings the paradigm of Westphalia's creation full circle: perhaps if Westphalia had not existed today, the Pope's Encyclical on climate change may actually have had real teeth and legitimacy to deal with the existential climate change threat the world now faces. In other words, *Laudato Si* if announced four-hundred years ago, would have had real global authority!

Westphalia set the tone for demarcation of borders worldwide. Borders that were largely defined as "might makes right". While the hegemonistic Sykes–Picot agreement (1916) contrived as a backstop to the chaos of the collapse of the Ottoman Empire by France and Britain and has been discussed many times in legal, world, and political histories, a look-back of Sykes–Picot extreme hubris and arrogance by established Westphalian powers imposing new and discrete boundaries subjectively on impoverished people groups can be well encapsulated in the subjective words of British politician Mark Sykes *"I should like to draw a line from the e in Acre to the last k in Kirkuk"*.[5]

Compounding these boundary and governance issues is the fact that these arbitrarily drawn nation-state borders continue to represent oppression to millions of people today. Even this human tragedy caused by the Sykes–Picot borders is clear to the world. Changing these decades-old international boundaries, that are supported by domestic political interests and international demand for stability is now virtually impossible. Elite interests are entrenched.

Therefore, the Westphalian system of a *"scaffolding of the worlds international order"* as Henry Kissinger put it, was designed to protect and ensure stability through inclusion and a common reference point of self-reinforcing, non-interference in the domestic affairs of like sovereign nations. We will hear more about this concept of non-interference throughout this book. It is a default position embraced by all nation-states today, though they obviously don't believe it, particularly when in regard to their economies.

For example, it is quite interesting to read Kissinger's arms-length and detached Westphalian dissection considering that this is from a former leader and Harvard University academic who had no intention of ever respecting the Westphalian system himself when dealing pragmatically with the *realpolitik* of the Cold War 1960s and 1970s era: US interference in Laos, Vietnam, Indonesia, East Timor, and Chile quickly come to mind. Stanford University professor Niall Ferguson has also written prolifically of Kissinger in two eras, the first, of Kissinger as academic, then secondly, as statesman, each with different mindsets.

The world as it existed in the mid-seventeenth century was a very big and intimidating place where natural borders were tightly defined. Country's frontiers were neatly separated by seas, rivers, deserts, straits, wilderness, or mountainous barriers. These borders largely contained inclusive cultural and religious differences and homogenous identities, where people largely looked and acted like each other. The New World of the Americas was barely 150 years old, Australia was largely undiscovered, and it would be yet another 200 years before David Livingstone penetrated the deepest African jungles.

This certainly does not hold true today, not in a cross-border, information intensive world, physically connected by cars, cellular phones, Wi-Fi, and aircraft. There was no wholesale economic migration as in Venezuela, or concept of mass immigration, as we have recently seen with the Syrian and Rohingya crises. People largely stayed where they were, for better or worse, with exception of religious persecution in reformation Europe, which saw Protestant separatists and Anabaptists either driven out or leave for the sake of their beliefs and lives. In short, the significant cross-border issues that effect today's world, namely climate change, migration, plastic pollution, resource depletion, cross-border poverty, air and sea "incursions", overfishing, etc. simply did not exist circa 1650. These are all pressing issues of the twenty-first century, presenting significant global challenges.

THE WESTPHALIAN CHOICE FALLACY

It has been suggested that people living in detestable conditions are free to "go" and move from one nation-state to another one by voting with their feet to avoid religious persecution, war, poverty, and other problems. This ridiculous and hubristic remedy is not so simple and very condescending, mostly as any free and unencumbered movement of people between nation-states realistically does not exist. For example, for a pig farmer in Cambodia or a banana peddler in Niger, obtaining foreign residence or passports can be a challenging mountain, both psychologically and economically. Even perchance when they do immigrate, they often find that little changes from one place to the next. As poor, newly arrived immigrants, they will be placed at the bottom of the social strata. In many cases, no matter what their previous occupation was. It is why we see Pakistani medical doctors driving taxi's in New York or Ukrainian physicists working as security guards in Australia, or Filipino engineers working as domestic helpers. Are their skills really that outdated and obsolete as some suggest, that being, their coming from developing, as opposed to developed countries? Perhaps, but the real reason may lie in labor opportunities or lack of them as fenced in by the Westphalian system. More of this is discussed in the "Pay for Passport" section of Chapter 4. Even with émigrés from more prosperous countries such as Germany or Korea, political stagnation may in large part be the result of the confines of the nation-state, which ensures the status quo as opposed to any sense of economic efficiency.

Consider that Westphalia politicizes nation-state services and forces conflicting political visions in diverse ethnic and religious populations leading to the path of dysfunction, inhibited social mobility, higher debt, and lower economic growth; it drives a wedge between people who otherwise may have little reason for animosity between themselves by creating an "us versus them" mindset of competition, not a spirit of cooperation. Enormous swaths of the global population are forced to support laws and policies they perhaps may detest simply because sovereign leaders can convince more than half the voting population in a so-called "Democratic" nation-state that preserving a miserable status quo is vital to their (meaning all) security or interests. As a response to this one-way road, separatist (such are Catalans in Spain) and large minority movements (Kurds in Iraq; Papuans in Indonesia) have gained traction and asserted a right to independence from central governments viewed as despotic, oppressive, or at the least ineffective and incompetent. The Arab Spring, the Scottish independence referendum, the Catalan and Taiwanese independence movements, Occupy protests in Hong Kong, the growth of Islamic terrorist networks such as ISIS and Al Qaeda, and nativist movements in Europe, Asia, and South America have all been the diffuse symptoms of a global power struggle exacerbated by fossilized nation-states that have remained unwilling or unable to ensure economic mobility, holistic change, and political voice at the expense of compromising those in power and wealth.

Today, in places like Singapore, South Korea, and Israel, it is easy to serenade to everyone who visits about a 'national cultural identity' (heterogenous in the former or homogenous in the latter two) if ones country is military protected by benefactor nations or by nations providing outside economic support such as finance or export markets. It is quite a different aspect however to piously preach about similar national culture in very corrupt, and war-torn countries, such as a Congo, Syria, Yemen, Sudan, Myanmar, Mali, or Tajikistan, which are surrounded by hostile neighbors or powerful outside nations who seek to lay claim on their territory directly, or by historical proxy, be it for natural resources, seaports, or any type of buffer state status. While Westphalia has historically derived considerable legitimacy from a legacy of "national culture", the definition of what that is, and what it portends to mean can readily change over time, as it has today. This is especially true in light of mass migration and exodus, territorial expansion, nondemocratic governance, and "beggar thy neighbor" economic policies. What this all means is that in the Information Age, the main pillar for the creation and conveyance of Westphalian legitimacy, "non-interference due to a cultural or ethnic identity", is severely compromised, if not outright nonsensical.

Westphalia's Relevance Has Expired

We consider that while Westphalia is now the "norm" among the 190 odd nations recognized by the United Nations, it is in light of all the above, developed from an ethnocentric Western ideological perspective, and a default position over the past four centuries. Nonetheless, it has also failed to deliver on today's most pressing cross-border issues besides climate change: poverty, inequality, and economic upheaval.

Sovereign State Roulette

Despite the proclaimed ideal of Westphalia, it is obvious that not all nation-states are created equal. There is a carefully weighted *realpolitik* game by big states versus small states that is used to justify influence in their regions (Russia and the Baltic, China and Southeast Asia) or even far away (the US, and.... one can fill in the blanks, most lately the Monroe Doctrine being resurrected with a problematic Venezuela or Ecuador seeking Russian and Chinese "support"). This is now considered in a new body of thought as contingent sovereignty[7] which took off after the 9/11 terrorist attacks in New York to justify then President George Bush's 2003 war on terror. If this is true, then all derivatives that flow from this logic will impact (and already have) the hemispheres. Consider a currency, a nuclear arms race, or extra-sovereign territorial claims. For example, the world runs on US dollars, the de facto "world currency" or medium of exchange. Every currency value on world markets is indexed against US dollars (never rubles, rupees, lira, or yen), oil, the worlds lifeblood is priced in dollars, bonds to rebuild and rejuvenate fallen nation-states are bought and sold in dollars. [This is important precedent that will be covered in detail in Chapter 6]. What this means is that Westphalia can conveniently be ignored when dealing in terms of economic necessity (or should we say, sovereignty becomes a secondary concern when dealing with the wealth of elites). Also due to this US dollar hegemony, a two-class system of sovereignty emerges: one for the US and another for everyone else.

So what about environmental necessity? It seems that ethereal and distant "environmental catastrophes" then don't take the same urgency as one's life savings. But if we are faced with a severely wounded and damaged planet, then having the economic band play on while the ship of humanity founders may simply not matter, though it's really that simple if one considers it.

Some has been written about the pros and cons of Westphalia as establishing the foundation for world secular governance, going back to Hegel. Writers have argued about the relevance then of Westphalia in regard to today's international problems (security, humanitarian activity, and the global economy) in other words it is taken as a "proof" that the Westphalian system must continue to exist in order to keep the world together. In fact one of the writers, obviously beholden to the concept of Westphalia as this unchangeable proof, ponders how an emergent ISIS fits within its framework. Oddly that is a similar argument used in the 1830s by many in the southern US to keep slavery intact and unquestioningly institutionalized with "positivist" legal decisions like Dred Scott (enforcing slave ownership even in strongly abolitionist states). Yet no one today would question slavery as a now illegitimate, but then it was a very real institution.

Writers like Kissinger, a noted war hawk and unabashed defender of US hegemony, (also defined by some now as 'US exceptionalism') clearly take the position that the Westphalian system was one of the more grandiose inventions in modern history, an equalized meeting of the best of minds. Yet, it would then be out of order to question the entire concept of "international law", *as international law at its core is in opposition to the entire exclusivity concept of Westphalia.* International law is about cross-border enforcement. Westphalia by its nature does **not** enshrine international law, but rather emasculates it if taken to its logical conclusion of non-interference and assured exclusivity. Treaties such as NATO and multilateral agreements like NAFTA have attempted to skirt around this realization with conflicting results. Simply, if nation-states and sovereignty as the ultimate denominator of non-interference are the norm, then international law must introduce itself as an uninvited interloper against exclusivity.

Exclusivity as accorded under the Westphalia arrangement also worked well until the very recent techno-industrial era began (post-1990) to infringe on national borders with other things such as digital currencies, air overflights, drone warfare, instantaneous communications, etc., or the "public goods" problems of refugees, territorial disputes, overfishing, and without argument the largest threat to it all, global warming.

Yet, none of the many writings have addressed the *Westphalian sovereignty effect* on climate change and its main causation: unrestrained burning of fossil fuels inside national borders. Therefore, the real issue perhaps is not to engage in the merits and pitfalls of having a Westphalia system (it simply "is what it is" and it exists as the only accepted world denominator of governance) but to realize that it is now a major impediment to the most pressing natural problem confronting modern human history since possibly the Black Plague of 1347 and arguably, superseding even the worst of man-made problem, nuclear proliferation from the atom bombs used in 1945. In other words, the Westphalian system, unchanged, is a root cause of the inability of the worlds' governments to collectively deal with issues. This cannot be overstated and will be covered more in detail in the next chapter.

Simply put, there is no legal mechanism (that is, no one-world authority) today based on that system that can coerce other nations into mechanisms that provide for solving global public goods (or public governance) problems. Of course the US, usually under cover of the United Nations, IMF, or NATO, indeed stemming from the Monroe doctrine itself in 1823, and particularly rooted in this regard to South America, has bent this mechanism to its own advantage to fit its national (mostly military) agenda; in other, weaker, sovereign countries such as with the Guantanamo Bay military fortification in Cuba, the Panama Canal, the South Korean DMZ, the Green Zone in Baghdad, and arguably the US base on Diego Garcia in the Indian Ocean, the last, which forcibly removed indigenous people groups (in a paper shuffle with the U.K. as they were "de-colonizing" their vast possessions in the 1960s). Small areas, no doubt, but still a blurring of the lines within a strict conceptual of Westphalia and exclusive domestic rights applied in a specific locale. This is a type of neocolonialism, as many would agree that the definition of traditional big power "colonialism" ended with British withdrawal from most of its large former colonies by the late 1940s, with decolonization due to strong nationalistic movements from the rest of the European countries (France, Spain, Portugal, and Holland) following suit by the early 1960s. Africa, with its many ugly and convoluted border disputes today, from Spanish Morocco to the Belgian Congo to Portuguese Angola, is also a legacy of this.

Further, we need to consider a value spectrum that all Westphalian systems utilize internally, they just don't proactively institutionalize it, largely due to political correctness concerns. By this we mean political, cultural, and anthropological values. Is the value of the society at large capitalistic or socialist? Is the culture individualistic like the US or collectivist like Korea? Is the society largely homogenous, like Japan, or heterogenous, like Singapore? This spectrum could be considered on an X-Y-Z planar

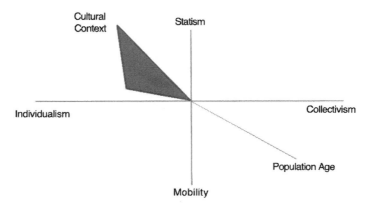

Fig. 1.1 Modern issues affecting viability of the Westphalian state: regional and international (Hickey adapted from G. Hofestede and F. Trompenaars studies)

axis, also noted that any values in a society are never absolute but plural-ist (for example, there are capitalists in socialist societies such as Sweden, as there are strong individuals in any collectivist society, such as China, there is statism in dynamic society, and changing people demographics in wealthy S. Korea and poorer India). This means that all motivations in proactively addressing issues will be different in each nation-state. All politics is local is the saying, and these factors must be addressed, as they get to the core of motivation. How motivated are these societies to solve the issues? That would seem to be a mute question, motivation meaning that they will collectively and uniformly accept a direct course of action? Outside dictatorships and autocratic governments, it probably won't hap-pen, and even in the most authoritative regimes, dissent is never far away. See Fig. 1.1.

The Twenty-First-Century Investiture Controversy: Digitalization Overcomes Westphalia

Let us take a step back in time a moment before Westphalia, and consider another aspect of power, or then realpolitik, in world history that receives scant interest today, the Investiture Controversy of the early middle ages. At that time, the Catholic church, in particular the Pope, spiritually ruled the European continent, he had the power to excommunicate ones soul to hell in the afterlife. These issues were a matter of life and death then. Someone cast adrift from the church became the walking dead, not to be dealt with or even considered as a person (similar to dealing with political correctness transgressions today). This of course spilled over into politics. Someone excommunicated had no legitimacy. The church also controlled many other walks of life. But who was invested with the power to appoint, or to consecrate, a pope in *this* life? In some ways this carries over today: secular governments arrogantly assume they are the full power in the world today, and that religion must be subservient to their allegiance. This is misguided. Westphalia was set up to counter the influence of religion on the nation-state. Namely, the influence of the Catholic church. But that did not mean religion was ever diminished or abolished. Protestantism was elevated to the level of state religion in Germany at that time. State religion still exists. Countries that declare themselves secular, such as Spain, Italy, Ireland, Indonesia, Malaysia, Saudi Arabia, the UAE, and Pakistan for example have their state religions written into their constitutions. They place religion as equal or even superior to their constitution.[8]

Essentially world events, such as climate change and the blockchain are forcing a consideration to the way that authority is derived, anticipated, and directed to deal with problems that affect ALL humanity not just ones in nation-states. Similar to Westphalia subsuming the rights of Popes and religion, the Digital Age may just well be the next logical step to subsume Westphalia. One might argue that if it is a purely secular authority, devoid of spiritualism, it may not carry the same *gravitas* as a spiritual concern. We consider then a "modern-day concordant", that is a melding of the minds between issues that concern the sovereign state and humanity at large. Maybe the spiritual is not the objective to be "minimized" any longer but rather the Westphalian entity. Conjecture? To be certain, but consider that during the Medieval Investiture Controversy, no one ever questioned the temporal power Popes and kings held, but rather the dynamics in getting there.

POSSIBLE METHODS OF GLOBAL CHANGE

Besides wars and direct military interventions, with clearly defined state actors, methods have been tried to incorporate global change that have an extra-sovereign effect outside the Westphalia framework with little success. A "*chipping at the edges*" approach if one wills when confronting a negative public goods problems, that is, a problem with negative effects on the planet that no one country wants to any take ownership of. When all "own it" no one owns it. Consider a few previous enfeebled attempts at overcoming sovereignty: A market-based approach (only works when all agree on world price), nonbinding agreements (generally unenforceable platitudes), treaties (only as robust as the weakest partner), holistic trade agreements (that can be loaded with all kinds of other agendas), supranational organizations (such as the Word Bank, IMF, or OECD, with only "suggestion power" on many issues).

Except for the market-based approach, with a set price honored by the markets under threat of contractual enforcement, each of the above methods has serious limitations. Crossing the "moat" of Westphalian sovereignty then is not subject to compromise with non-interested parties. We can see this clearly with the Greece versus EU fiscal drama in 2015. The EU, a regional organization, could not penetrate Greek sovereignty deeply enough to force serious domestic changes (restructuring) in its member state. However, the banks could. Conversely, abolishing Greece (then so-called "Grexit") could start a domino effect across the entire EU, with future countries threatening to leave under financial duress. The EU experiment has in effect been about giving up some sovereignty for a greater regional good, but without a financial or fiscal union (all in economic unison with transparent, non-deviating economic budgets) it has been severely compromised.

World Markets and the Dollar

Throughout recent Industrial Age history (post-1800), commerce has been considered the lifeblood and soothing balm in preventing and alleviating worldwide conflicts. To that end, a market-based approach is considered the best remedy when dealing with Westphalian governance. Consider the *Dell Theory of Capitalist Peace* espoused by NYT sage (or shill?) Thomas Friedman, that *"no two countries with McDonalds (or Dell Computer dealers) go to war"*. Yet, this very idealized construct of symbiotic economies may no longer hold water. One can order a Big Mac and fries in Ukraine and Russia, or in any of the claimant states surrounding the South China Sea, or in Venezuela and Colombia. Yet, it doesn't mean that they get along, or may not be on the verge of war with each other.

NYT writer Thomas Friedman's globalization tomes (The World is Flat, The Lexus and the Olive Tree), etc., don't mention anything about Westphalian system push and pull factors that enable cross-border trade, and waters down significant political manipulation of finance (devaluations, quantitative easing, negative interest rates, etc.), mostly for jobs creation. For example, the world is dealing today with an extreme divergence, versus a convergence, in interest rate policies and currency values among various countries. Yet, the world's undeniable reference currency for all is the US dollar. Everything is referenced with the dollar. This is economic asymmetry (difference in expectations and methods employed) and is causing havoc in world currencies. The recent currency declines of all commodity producing countries such as New Zealand, Nigeria, Kazakhstan, and Malaysia, are all which are linked to the US dollar, is notable.

GLOBAL WARMING

Climate change is caused by the nations' unmitigated burning of fossil fuels for energy. It is also the poster-child of Westphalian impotence with public goods problems. Current government frameworks allow certain "sovereign" countries to spew emissions of mostly coal (such as India, Indonesia, and China) without any restraint, or threat of outside interference, all in the name of economic growth/catching up with developed countries, electrification expansion, self-reliance, etc. The excuses are plentiful, the teeth of enforcement largely nonexistent. The Kyoto, Copenhagen, La Paz, and now Paris climate conferences become meaningless charades by domestic politicians with photo ops of international counterparts, who can't (and won't) sacrifice the economic growth that keeps them in power for any distant and ethereal public goods dilemma that no one owns. For example, China recently stated that it underestimated its coal emissions by nearly 1 billion tons of CO_2 which is more than the entire yearly emissions of all of industrial powerhouse Germany. It is estimated that 2015/6 peat fires in Indonesia to clear land for palm oil plantations emitted as much CO_2 as the entire US yearly industrial output. As there is no binding world consensus, there is no transgression or international sanction, again, it is what it is.

The irony is that while Westphalian adherence allows countries to hide behind the veneer of sovereignty and handwringing when dealing with a global warming public goods problem, they have had no qualms about uniting forcibly (usually under US coercion and financial sanctions it should be pointed out) against an Iran or North Korea trying to develop a nuclear weapon, or most recently, uniting to tackling the problem of ISIS/ISIL in the Mideast (again with US carrots and sticks attached) or in dealing immediately with a public threat problem such as SARS, MERS, or Ebola. Nonetheless, unchecked global warming is as much of a catastrophic threat to all humanity and world economies as a nuclear armed Iran, Syrian/Iraqi-based ISIL terrorists, or pandemic in the Central African Republic.

Plastic Waste

The world has a major garbage problem that is manifesting itself in the worlds oceans, with individual nation-states kicking the ball to and fro. The world is addicted to cheap polystyrene derived from oil to make all the accessories, bags, and liquid containers it needs. Nonetheless it can take hundreds of years to degrade plastic waste; and burning it creates even more noxious and hazardous air pollution. Developing countries such as China and Malaysia have recently banned the importation of this waste to protect their own exclusive environments. The issue with plastic waste is that as it breaks down into smaller and smaller components, it has the potential to move up the food chain, with health unknown consequences to animals and humans.

World Finance and Westphalia

Or consider the US mandated FATCA (foreign account tax compliance act), which forces any bank extra-territorially but with a US presence (for example, Santander Bank is largely a Spanish bank but with some branches in the US) or even using US dollars (such as the world football FIFA corruption scandal, where merely using US dollars that have transited a US bank led to US government/FBI corruption charges) to find all US citizens or residents who have foreign investments or involvement abroad to enforce overall US taxation policy. If these banks worldwide don't ascribe to FATCA they could lose US market access and thus US dollar access, the same for any entity using US dollars. **We can clearly see then that Westphalia can be overcome if the political will is as determined and cocksure as when the US tackles financial crimes**. Climate change and severe immigration issues should take much the same precedence.

Additionally, in regard to global warming, any market-based (or commercial) mechanism that requires setting a "price for carbon" must be actually enforced by all the markets in unison. If not, leakage, enforcement gaps, and noncompliance immediately occurs, accompanied by extreme volatility and price manipulation (should the price be $10, $15, or $50 per metric ton of CO_2 emissions?) will ensue as has previously happened on the European exchanges for carbon credits. This has been the biggest problem all along with pricing for carbon emissions and creating a carbon credit exchange: enforcement. Oddly, all carbon prices are discussed in US dollars, as is oil, meaning in a world reserve currency that will not fluctuate.

What "the markets" really mean by enforcement however is that of a final arbiter, or a global sheriff, in this case the US court system, that will enforce their contracts, investigate corruption, and discipline wayward participants in that said market with severe financial and criminal penalties for any wrongdoing. Use of the dollar can also de facto realize this. The EU cannot do this, nor Japan, nor the UK, nor Australia, only the US, with its world reserve currency dollar can pull this arrangement off, with the markets clearly obeying and responding accordingly. The US, again due to domestic political forces, has a strong party disagreement that does not wish to lend credence to the entire aspect of global warming, lest it effect the economy and profitability of certain fossil-fuel intensive industries: coal, oil, utility companies, plastic extrusions, that garner deep support from the conservative politicians.

MIGRANTS AND REFUGEES

The issue of political refugees and economic migrants is not new. Many countries, not just Germany with its waves of Middle-Eastern migrants, have trouble truly sorting out who is who, that is, which person or family is deserving of asylum and who is not? Harvard Professor Michael Teitelbaum has researched international migration for over 30 years and, among the motivations for why people migrate and become refugees, mostly the economic incentive. People will put up with political authoritarianism as long as the money is flowing. Political strife causes economic activity to shrivel. People migrate then to better their own personal and family circumstances, not to cast votes for elite politicians in distant lands promising an ambiguous concept of "freedom" or to protest against military invasions. Teitelbaum's 1980 prediction that immigration and refugee issues would become the foremost troubling issue of our time has been very prescient. Teitelbaum, and later Nobel laureate Douglas North, have demonstrated that economics and politics cannot be neatly drawn and squared in separate boxes to tick or issues to contain. There are gray areas, many complicated by contradictory policies, that give rise to rent-seeking opportunities by those in charge, that is forcing a market price for any political boundary that people, are willing to pay to cross.

Territorial Disputes

China was never a party in the original Westphalian European table setting of the seventeenth century but rather, a long-suffering country at the hands of colonialism from the great powers itself in the nineteenth century. Nonetheless, it has gone one hundred eighty degrees towards Westphalia starting in 1949 with its modern founding under Chairman Mao Zedong: China now feels very entitled to catch up and right past abuses (at the hands of the same European countries and with Japan in particular), with its roaring economic and military clout, and tightly embracing Westphalia with its mantra of non-interference in others affairs, nonetheless itself engaging in manipulation of Westphalia for sovereign salami slicing of territory with its regional neighbors. We can see this playing out today in their island land grab, upgrading, militarization, and neighborly derring do, in the South China Seas. Various uninhabited islets, in many cases, just rocks, are being claimed by which China justifies on a millennial "historic" basis, long before Westphalia even existed. The Communist Party and Standing Committee make it clear through their various mouthpieces that the islands are an "inalienable part of China" (similar to Taiwan), and that any "treaty" defined by Western powers (such as the 1951 *Treaty of San Francisco* which demarcated Japans and East Asia's borders post-WWII) simply does not apply to them. China enjoys using Westphalia to its advantage, and quickly disowning it when not.

If successful in their South China Sea endeavors, expect China also to eventually lay claim to other places, such as the Antarctic which has no one sovereign protector, only a UN mandate in place, or Mongolia, which was forcibly ceded to the USSR's sphere of influence after WWII under Josef Stalin's tenure. In short, China will bend Westphalian rules by pushing the envelope as much as it can for its own advantage, and lacking US involvement, no other sovereign power in itself can 'contain' this. The US has also set a bad precedent for this by setting up military installations in the before mentioned places. Chinese territorial aspirations might also be construed as a "public goods" dilemma facing/threatening the world under a "might makes right" scenario.

SPACE JUNK

Recently, India cheered shooting down a satellite in low orbit with a military missile. That was cause for their cheer, but not for the worlds! The debris field created now poses a danger to the international space station, and any future space exploration efforts. Space junk can travel faster than a bullet, and can destroy or cripple satellites, payloads, or space stations in its path. Their Westphalian exclusivity now creates clear dangers for other neighbors, and mans colonization of space itself, which may be a potential breakwater for ensuring mankind's long-term survival. The debris field is just the beginning, what about colonies on the moon or Mars? Will the bubble of Westphalia be extended far and wide to places far removed from their original sovereign intent, in order to protect diplomatic niceties?

SO WHOM DOES THE WESTPHALIAN SYSTEM REALLY BENEFIT TODAY?

We live on an overpopulated world with significant people (now 7.2 billion) and environmental problems that will not magically go away no matter how hard certain nations seek to wall themselves off or ignore reality. Pollution and climate change do not stop at borders with visas in tow, and increasingly refugees to the US, EU, and Oceana are not stopping at borders either. The Westphalian world of 350 plus years ago, was a very different place with very different parameters, mindsets, and visions. Nonetheless, while the faces and names changed over time, the original issues intended of elite actors maintaining power and wealth are still there, from then barons, knights, and dukes to the entrenched central bankers, military officers, and CEOs of today. Westphalia, like the Magna Carta, was never designed or created for the rights of the many, but rather to consolidate and protect the rights of the few within its exclusivity arrangements. Similar to spokes on a bicycle wheel, the integrity and construct of the Westphalian system is reinforced internally, by elite pillars of self-interest.

AN ECONOMISTS VIEW OF WESTPHALIA

Douglas North, the 1990 Nobel laureate in economics for his theory on the "natural state" of human existence, whereby, most of today's world still is defined by personal transactions and favoritism to form contracts and enforce agreements. The Westphalian system keeps this status quo going. If there is no gainsharing or democratic channels between all groups in a given society, North's theory suggests, those excluded will rebel and seek greener pastures elsewhere. This is the situation in Syria, Libya, Venezuela, and Yemen today, with civil wars, endemic poverty, and no economic opportunity on the horizon, people leave. North argues that the economy and politics are inextricably intertwined: All political problems are rooted in economic ones and vice versa. Enfranchisement and empowerment of competing groups are required for a sustainable and "open society". Only a handful of countries have ever reached this level of empowerment. Without this societal advancement to full transparency, elites will dictate to all.

If taken to a further proof level, then the Westphalian system per se actually sits in opposition to full democracy. Democracy considers the rights of the many (also others rights, even outside domestic borders if we consider an idealized Athenian or Swiss founding system of the fourteenth century). This is not a new concept, consider that some have insisted on allowing the world to vote in US presidential elections since US domestic decisions, in particular about the US military, finance, and the dollar, have a real and pronounced effect on peoples lives and their countries all over the world. Yet, hypocritically, the US founders, on their own accord, also refused to let popular elections define a president. Consider Donald Trump, who won the electoral vote in the 2016 US Presidential election, but lost by over a staggering 2 million votes in the popular vote. Thus, even in the US, despite piously preaching "free" elections to the rest of world (and vigorously funding at times intrusive democracy initiatives in newly emerging economies), the rights of *their* elites are preserved and upheld through various institutionalized mechanisms. This is also exactly what also led to the formation of the Magna Carta and Westphalia: elite actions.

Structural Reforms: Heavy Lifting

Generally, structural reforms refer to restructuring labor and workforces. In our case, structural reform refers to restructuring the entire concept of sovereignty and governance on a tiny and environmentally vulnerable planet, approaching 10 billion people by 2050, with simply far too many mouths to feed, all aspiring to very unrealistic Western consumption based standards of living patterns as advertised on social media. Growing consumption that underpins economic activity but also fuels global warming and trans-migrational problems. Unfortunately, wealth gaps and disparity continues to grow around the world, while overall (according to the UNDP) most people have been lifted out of abject poverty the last 20 years, the elites and certain monied interests are clearly benefitting from this seventeenth-century system that enforces their rights over the planets relatively limited capacity.

A critical structural reform today would be in dismantling the Westphalian system and enjoining a new conference, that also fully considers the rights and cultural diversity of Africa, South American and Asian peoples. Idealistic? Hardly, consider that the first Westphalian Peace in 1648 was attended to address almost the *same issues* that are facing the world today: Endless wars, political turmoil, financial upheaval, and the high mortality rates (or in today's metric: endemic poverty) that they fostered. But at that time, only the European continent was the focus. The development of South and North America was in their infancy, Asia was still stuck in feudal/dynastic systems or colonized.

Full Circle

If the point of Westphalia was to bring regional exclusivity to differing ideas, cultures, and religions, in the then *nouveau* concept of "nation-state", that ideal is being put to the test today. Simply, a single claim and modus to truth and universal rule may be necessary to return to what was left off in 1648 and restarted in this twenty-first century, namely, one definitive authority to set the tone however politically unpalatable that may be, or perhaps using the highly contentious words of "one-world governance" contexted with the digital age.

Expiry Date

If Westphalia was yesterday's grand solution to wars and religious conflict, it is now today's problem, specifically in regard to global public goods issues. The geographical monopoly on governance was perhaps easier to maintain a long ago time before industrialization and globalization happened. Now however, this course is largely irreversible; with the seemingly unstoppable move toward digital interconnectedness, the world has become increasingly smaller through international trade, instant and borderless communications channels like the Internet, cheap transport, and large-scale migration. People are now enmeshed across borders, resulting in desires less defined by their geographical origin or location. In essence, this means that over time, nation-states and their transnational counterparts such as the United Nations (UN), NATO, and are becoming less relevant, in tandem with nation-states due to being built on the same outdated, top-down, monopolistic foundation. The Westphalia system has an "expiry" date, which has long since arrived. Why should 7.2 billion people on Earth only be able to choose between perhaps a handful of different types of governance and without the freedom of movement and wealth protection between those options? This limited choice of governance systems does not make sense in modern times, and in particular in our cross-border digital era. The Westphalian nation-state is a form of governance that has grown outdated, and which is now impeding, not enabling, human social and economic evolution and progress.

Apples and Oranges

Our world is more fractured with polarized political dysfunction than ever before, and yet, at the same time, more interconnected with instantaneous social media and data (i.e. AI, the sharing economy, blockchain). Divergence and convergence coexist! The world is simply overloaded with information that needs to be understood. Westphalia seems more of a friction to any information flow than an enhancer. Slow reaction times could be catastrophic. If one reads an issue of the *Economist*, Wall Street Journal, or *Financial Times*, or even their news on the Internet, every story, argument, problem, and statistics table is denominated in the context of the nation-state, whether huge like Canada or tiny, like the Maldives. Yet, as previously mentioned, not all nation-states carry the same gravitas, but Westphalia, in its natural form, absurdly considers them as all "equals" at the table. A rationale that has been force fed to everyone the past 75 years since the end of WWII with the development of post-WWII multilateral institutions at Bretton-Woods.

It certainly becomes a nonparametrical and lopsided argument if one compares statistical yardsticks of a behemoth landmass country such as China to minute Monaco, or an overpopulated, heterogenous India to sparsely populated homogenous Iceland, or a poverty-stricken Congo to an *Uber* wealthy Japan. The tremendous imbalances that exist in huge nation-states create an unbalanced non-parametric incongruence to any statistical analysis. It may be better to examine, perhaps, *certain regions* of giant countries, in some proximity, such as comparing and contrasting Shanghai to nearby South Korea, or Bavaria to Northern Italy to understand more regional economic growth issues influences, or further, domestic development issues. Many consider Italy as two countries: the industrialized and affluent northern Italy, and the agrarian and poor southern Italy, rather than blanket macroeconomic studies that aggregate a nation on unbalanced terms. These overall "averages" can enhance or dilute the narratives by using extreme data. Better comparables are in order, and necessary to serve constituencies, in particular by the supranational organizations like the UN and WB that seek to box countries.

OPTIONS? ABOUT URGENCY AND PERSPECTIVE

Alternatives to the current Westphalian system are certainly a prescient question, if anything, further allusion to a one-world government cannot be ruled out, simply because the nation-state concept rooted in Westphalia is powerless to deal with horrible public goods issues as repeatedly aforementioned on a global level. Consider the odd historical paradigms: no US slave owner in say, 1825 ante-bellum Virginia gave much thought to any "optional system" to their "peculiar institution", similarly, no denizen of Omsk in the Soviet Union in 1972, gave much thought to "forming democratic governance". Nonetheless, those systems did in fact change, both violently and radically, within a relatively short time. As Ernest Hemingway wrote in *The Sun Also Rises*, change always comes *"gradually, then suddenly"*. Globalism tries to couch itself in the Hegel nuances of culture, religion, and ethnicity, by creating a state as everything inference, but that is a smokescreen. Globalism is about money and elite interests, and always has been, from wherever they be, usurping traditional pillars of the equanimous nation-state.

DISMANTLEMENT

A new system is called for to replace Westphalia, perhaps scrapping the concept of the nation-state then altogether (however radical that may seem). Westphalia has came full circle in its inception and original purpose. It simply creates an obstacle in today's information intensive and cross-border world by blindly propagating its existence as if there is no other alternative. Nothing is indispensable, nor sacred, if humanities very survival is at hand. Westphalia should not be considered an abstract proof of an accepted denominator in itself, beyond criticism or adjustment, the world simply can't afford it in the twenty-first century.

CHINA

China, the worlds second largest economy, was a dynastic order in the seventeenth century with vassaldoms, and not an original adherent to the Westphalia treaty. China's deep feudal and dynastic past for many centuries promoted a regional hegemony. Despite its loud and pious proclamations of "*non-interference in others affairs*", China actually interferes in other nations affairs quite robustly via its powerful economic investment largesse and extra-territorial "*salami slicing*" methods and claims, as in the South China Sea and against militarily weaker regional neighbors such as Vietnam, Kyrgyzstan, the Philipines, or Laos. China presents a case study of the world's emerging superpower, that has usurped, some might say co-opted Westphalia past its original intent and purpose, by creating secularist governance above dynasticism and ethnicism in a guise for deep-state control, which rarely presents alternative information to a controlled population. China is a country governed (as are most developed countries) by engineers, not lawyers (as in the West), where mathematical, discrete, finite solutions outweigh variable social ones that are open to criticism.

SUMMARY

It is difficult to see how diversity alone can congeal into any "synergetic" force to confront today's cross-border threats to humanity without an overarching directive. Otherwise, sovereign governments, hiding behind their exclusive Westphalian curtains, will continue to default, debate, deny, bicker, obfuscate, and distort what real actions needing to be taken to confront global problems. Countries that embrace their sovereignty with positions of isolationism, as with the US (for example, not a signatory on the UN's convention on war crimes, International Criminal Court, or on the proliferation and use of cluster bombs) or like China with an extreme stand on non-interference of "internal affairs" (broadly interpreted) especially in regions such as Taiwan, Tibet and Xinjiang (the latter two with very non- ethnic Chinese populations seeking self-determination), become part of the bigger problem not the solution, and are perhaps the biggest threat to getting to a consensus on pressing decisions. Without addressing the most serious threats facing mankind in a unified and in an enforceable manner, little will change. The Westphalian system, a product of a bygone era that dealt with religious issues, today threatens humanity with its old framework by failing to incorporate transnational issues requiring a collectively enforced effort.

As such this book follows three consistently interwoven themes in regard to Westphalia, triangulated from a philosophical (Hegel), political (Kissinger, Marx) and economic (North, Teitelbaum, Rothbard) perspectives. These three themes are presented in the next ten chapters as follows:

1. Climate change is a real and looming global problem humanity faces. Nonetheless, humanity is boxed in by Westphalia, or is mistakenly assuming that technological innovation will somehow emerge to solve the issue at the 11th hour. This is cognitive dissonance. Westphalia is powerless to solve this issue, works in opposition to it, and any technological wherewithal will not magically coalesce on a noncoherent demand. It never has without a demand driver.

2. As an extension to the above, Westphalia is not only powerless to solve climate change, it is anathema to all public goods problems, and one could say it "gets in the way". Westphalia is built on exclusivity and individual nation-state initiative to protect vested interests inside that nation-state. Whether it be climate change, plastic trash, universal income equality, cross-border immigration, influenza pandemics, space debris, or fishing rights, Westphalia simply cannot address these issues, and clinging to Westphalia blindly (such as China, India and the US do), worsens them. As an aside, cross-border treaties, multilateralism, and international conventions are limited in their scope and power and, like a chain, are only as strong as the weakest agreement. Big data, AI, and the blockchain, only serve to highlight Westphalian weakness, not strength, when dealing with world economic trends and borderless issues. Nonetheless, nation-states will cling to their Westphalian dissonance to avoid any crucial internal restructuring with their institutions for political stability.

3. The US dollar is the world's ascripted currency. All economic life under the economic euphemism "foreign reserves" revolve around the dollar if not directly, such as in dollar holdings, dollar pegs or dollarized bonds, then indirectly, as in exchange rates, devaluations, factoring, bond markets, fossil fuels, and import/export input and output pricings. The dollar really is king as there is no alternative

on the horizon anyone either trusts, has the availability of (liquidity), or will invest in for the long haul. Essentially then the US dollar is the global currency, which has good and bad implications, as we shall see. It is not even de facto. **It is preeminent**. Westphalia has thus acknowledged the dollar as the world's currency, since all nation-states rely on it. The dollar horse pulls the world's economic wagon. Any country without access to US dollars is economically doomed. As a silver lining, and as we shall see in Chapter 10, the world's ongoing dollar addiction could possibly be leveraged for a greater good then. The world craves the US dollar, despite all the US economic and social issues, as it is the only currency it knows in the twenty-first century. That paradigm will not change anytime soon, Bitcoin, the Chinese yuan, and others are only distant runners in the economic race.

Coda

As a coda, one may consider that in the world today the aspiration trend has been on course to creating even *more* Westphalian systems, not less (South Sudan, Kosovo, West Morocco, Abkhazia, Scotland, Catalonia, perhaps even a new Kurdistan or East Syria, etc.). Nonetheless, this would seem to exacerbate the problems of mass migration, closed borders, currency wars, and buffer-states. Dismantling Westphalia and seeking agglomeration of governance, as opposed to atomization, may present a crucial turning point in world politics, but first the systemic underpinnings of Westphalia need to be addressed and examined with critical inspection. That won't be easy. As history has shown, the Westphalian system was never designed to solve pressing global problems, as it considered borders inwardly, to but rather to keep elites well protected in individual, domestically oriented, socioeconomic power structures that they control, certainly not the *hoi polloi*!

Notes

1. Alvise Contarini was the Venetian interlocutor at Westphalia, a role he had assumed as early as 1641.
2. Andreas Osiander has written that the entire premise of Westphalia is misunderstood, but it is a minority opinion.

3. Credit for this Hegel discourse is given to Professor Tim Huson, a Hegel scholar at GDUFS who spent long hours and time explaining to me Hegel's position on both Westphalia and the state. Westphalia was Germanic in context and Hegel arguably Germany's most noted philosopher.
4. Kissinger writes at length about the political history of Westphalia in his 2014 book "World Order".
5. Werke 12, Lectures on the philosophy of history, pp. 514–520.
6. *A Line in the Sand*. James Barr, Simon and Schuster, 2011, Chapter 1.
7. Elden, S. (2006) Contingent Sovereignty, Territorial Integrity and the Sanctity of Borders. *SAIS Review* XXVI (1).
8. Consider that Indonesia in 2018, claiming to be a secular government, jailed the former mayor for 2 years for blaspheming Islam. Ireland until recently outlawed abortion based on the state religion of Catholicism.

BIBLIOGRAPHY

Al-Kassimi, K. (2015) The Obsolescence of the Westphalian Model and the Return to a Maximum State of Exception. *Journal of Political Science and Public Affairs* S2: 007.

Bartleson, J. (April 2006) The Concept of Sovereignty Revisited. *European Journal of International Law* 17 (2): 463–474.

Budge, I. (2001) Direct Democracy. In Paul A. B. Clarke and Joe Foweraker (eds.), *Encyclopedia of Political Thought*. Taylor & Francis. ISBN 978-0-415-19396-2.

Bull, H. (1985) *The Expansion of International Society*. Oxford: Oxford University Press.

Croxton, D. (1999) The Peace of Westphalia of 1648 and the Origins of Sovereignty. *International History Review* 21 (3): 569–591.

Ferguson, N. (2016) *Kissinger, 1923-1968: The Idealist, Vol. 1*. London: Penguin Books.

Ford Record Sales: http://www.ft.com/cms/s/0/975d45f8-0d37-11e6-ad80-67655613c2d6.html. Retrieved on July 2018.

Friedman, T. (2007) *The World Is Flat*, Douglas and McIntyre (2013) Limited, p. 421.

Hegel, G. F. W. (1795) Werke 12, *Lectures on the Philosophy of History*, pp. 514–520.

Hemingway, E. (1926) *The Sun also Rises*. New York: Scribner and Sons.

Janis, M. S. (1994) Sovereignty and International Law: Hobbes and Grotius. In R. St. J. Macdonald (ed.), *Essays in Honour of Wang Tieya*. Dordrecht, The Netherlands: Kluwer Academic Publishers. pp. 391, 393.

Kissinger, H. (2014) *World Order*. London: Touchstone, pp. 3–5.

Mihatsch. (2014) A Post-Westphalian Caliphate? Deconstructing ISIS Ambitions. Accessed 10/3 in: http://www.worldcrunch.com/syria-crisis-1/a-post-westphalian-caliphate-deconstructing-isis-ambitions.

Nordhaus, W. (2005) *Paul Samuelson and Global Public Goods.* Yale University Essay, 5/5.

North, D. (2006) A Conceptual Framework for Interpreting Recorded Human History. NBER Working Paper No. 1279.

Osiander, A. (2001). Sovereignty, International Relations, and the Westphalian Myth. *International Organization* 55 (2): 251–287.

Pinkard, T. (2002) *German Philosophy 1760–1860: The Legacy of Idealism.* Cambridge: Cambridge University Press.

Safanova, S. (2012) Relevance of the Westphalian System to the Modern World. Accessed 9/29 in: http://www.articlemyriad.com/relevance-westphalian-system-modern-world-sasha-safonova/.

Soros, G. (2000) *Open Society Reforming Global Capitalism Reconsidered.* Perseus Books.

Stiglitz, J. (2015) *The Great Divide.* London: Allen Lane.

Teitlebaum, M. (1980) Right Versus Right. *Foreign Affairs* 59 (1): 21–59.

Uchida, H. (2015) *Marx's Grundrisse and Hegel's Logic.* Terrell Carber (ed.). London: Routledge.

Zakaria, Fareed. (1994) Culture Is Destiny: Conversation with Lee Kuan Yew. *Foreign Affairs* 73 (2).

CHAPTER 2

Climate Change and Westphalia

*Climate Change is an ethereal and abstract public
goods problem that simply no one wants to "own"*

THE WESTPHALIAN ROOM

The historical and systematic narrative of world governance and human history needs to be understood from a paradigm of which to deal with today's most critical of all pan-border issues, climate change. The Westphalian system or treaty set in 1648, on which rests the modern foundation of all national sovereignty via its key pillar of exclusivity, simply can no longer deliver on its original "peace mandate" in today's information age. Westphalia is a contrivance of another age, that then faced its own peculiar issues of renaissance and reformation, issues that are no longer pertinent today in a highly secularized world. As long as these systemic underpinnings are ignored, unacknowledged, and not addressed as a root cause of pressing global governance issues, a constant back and forth with yet to be realized technological innovation, who ultimately pays for climate change, and its public goods ownership dilemma will continue *ad nauseum* with no clear answer, or any real way forward. This is more than academic semantics. Global climate agreements like the Paris Accord and most recently, COP25 in Madrid, are very limited in their enforcement effectiveness and scope due specifically to the Westphalia sovereign

© The Author(s) 2020
W. Hickey, *The Sovereignty Game*,
https://doi.org/10.1007/978-981-15-1888-1_2

exclusivity arrangement. How the problem of climate change is framed, addressed, and confronted is what really confounds humanity today. Climate change is not an abstract problem, though to many, it appears to be. Atmospheric data, melting arctic ice, increased frequency of storms and wildfires, desertification, and overall biological changes with forests and insect migrations have demonstrated that anthropogenic climate change is a very real and looming threat to all humanity.

Of interest here is that many leaders, scholars, and business people put the mistaken assumption in play that "world governments", (most writers use the terms "we" and "our" responsibility) will suddenly awaken to and embrace the threat of climate change as equally responsible partners in the good fight. Nothing could be further from the truth. That may well work in wartime, when allies coalesce to fight textual and visual "bad guys" in the form of a Nazi uniform, a belligerent African junta, or Japanese Kamikaze planes against a context of world mayhem. But in the case of global warming, the textual "bad guy" becomes an ethereal, abstract, actor (rising sea levels, uncontrolled wildfires, superstorms, record heatwaves, and melting glaciers) and with all very real, damaging consequences dictating life or death to those affected. Further, some countries have leaders, beyond US President Donald Trump, that also claim climate change is a distant problem, to be dealt with in next generations, thus becoming a "you problem", not a "we problem".

INTERNAL CONTRADICTIONS

Nonetheless there really is no "we" in fighting climate change in a Westphalian lexicon. Today's countries: developing and developed, autocratic and democratic, rich importer and poor exporter, religious fundamentalist or secular, also face far too many internal contradictions to address climate change as one-coherent voice, in fact, it's impossible. Societies begin to work at cross purposes, redundancy and contradiction becoming the result. For example, Australia wants green initiatives but is one of the world's largest coal exporters. Germany seeks a low carbon society, but has allowed brown coal to retake much of their electricity grid to support jobs. Indonesia has great expectations of becoming a responsible player with the Paris accords, but at the same time not only exports thermal coal, but lets the Chinese build gigantic coal-fired plants that dot the Java landscape in the time being.

What the Westphalian system *does do* however, is allow these same countries to default to do nothing, or take weakly conceived positions that firstly enable support for their economic activity, which 88% of the world's economy is predicated on continued use ([and abuse] such as with government subsidies) of fossil fuels. This predicate to the carbon addiction as an economic driver fits the total bill: Fuel for mobility (planes, trains, and automobiles), heating (coal, diesel, and natural gas powered) and poly-vinyls (plastic bags, bottles, and Apple iPhones). The world runs on fossil fuels, and the Westphalian system, with its main pillar of the "exclusivity of sovereignty" abets all the countries in doing so. This complicity is universal and beyond question.

The science behind climate change, leading to global warming, is incontrovertible. The process of burning fossil fuels like oil and coal release carbon dioxide which amplifies the impact of the greenhouse effect as populations, in particular in developing countries, grow. People didn't cause the greenhouse effect by using fossil fuels: it's a natural process in which gasses released in the atmosphere trap the sun's heat and cause warming. Without this effect, the Earth would be much colder and, perhaps, not nearly as hospitable to live on. Nonetheless, oil, coal, and natural gas are simply too crucial to our existence to simply remove them and are here to stay. As BP's Bernard Looney, chief executive of the energy giant's upstream division, puts it, "[I]n almost every scenario – oil and gas together are forecast to represent greater than 40% of the energy mix in 2040". Keep in mind that as world population densities grow, so do the overall numbers of use, even though actual or gross percentages used may decline. That is a real problem.

There is no "knocking about the bushes" with this issue. The year 2017, was the hottest recorded year in human history since the Industrial Age began in the early 1850s, and with 2019 now recently ranked as the second hottest year in recorded history. As of this writing, 400 ppm of CO_2 has already been recorded as average for 2017, with 2018 closely behind. These are all factual issues. The world cannot be allowed to burn carbon banks (the planets yet unused stores of oil, gas, and coal reserves that are still in the ground) unmitigated and without consequence. Yet, that is what is exactly continuing to happen, and all country's economies are betting on it. For example, consider the much publicized economic joy a nation receives when a new deposit of oil is found. Renewables are an emerging technology, less than 10% of worlds energy usage at best, and far too costly for developing countries despite the public relations campaigns by vendors. Further, renewables are not able to provide the consistent baseload of power that are guaranteed with fossil fuels (Fig. 2.1).

There is also no sense in rehashing all the technical climate change issues that have been passed on or ignored by respective politicians....

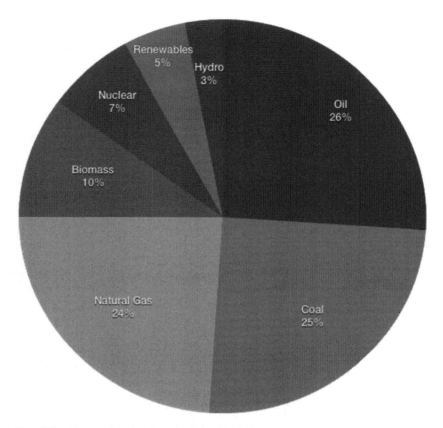

Fig. 2.1   Energy baseload outlook in 2040 (*Source* IEA, 2018)

everywhere. The problems with global warming and its causation are now well understood by everyone, including fossil-fuel companies and even world militaries. It is no longer disputable science, but indisputable reality. Bill McKibben's 2012 seminal article *"Global Warming's Terrifying New Math"* presciently displays the climate change problem in very good layspeak, his yardsticks (350 ppm, 2 degrees Celcius, 565 gigatons, etc.) and the repercussions of inaction are quite clear. Simply too much carbon burning overwhelms the planets natural capacity for CO_2 absorption. While the science is indisputable, the economics not so much. As with pouring more and more sugar into a glass of hot water in that an overload eventually will not dissolve, a continuing buildup of CO_2 expands in the atmosphere, distorting the earth's natural absorption and cooling processes, and wreaking havoc with weather patterns. The science, again, is indisputable, yet the fossil fuel band plays on. The emotional appeals featuring polar bears, melting Alpine glaciers, submerged islands in the Pacific, or flooded New York City streets are well meaning, but the facts are already registered. It is politicians locked in their Westphalian systems of power and money refusing to act in unison. Action will also require wholesale changes in everyone's energy consumption. Simply put, we're not there yet. There is no sense in discussing renewables *ad nauseum* either, because their front-end costs, without large subsidies are simply too expensive for most of the developing world to power their grids. Coal is cheaper and plentiful, as is natural gas, which is also a fossil fuel, despite politically correct energy markets presenting it as a 'transition energy' source, between fossil fuels and renewables. Developing countries will use their Westphalian exclusivity to default every time, as they have before, and will continue to do so.

To put this into perspective, consider global events: Ford Motor company is announcing record sales of SUVs in the US, Toyota is expanding into Africa, China is going to bring several hundred coal-fired plants online in the next 20 years, and in all Asia as part of its financing in its new "Asian Infrastructure Development Bank", Indonesia is expanding huge airports to accommodate more traveler's in its huge archipelago, Exxon discovers a huge oil field off Guyana's coast, Brasil hopes that its new "pre-salt" deep sea oil strike developed with the Norwegian oil giant, Statoil will power its corrupt and weak economy ahead, BP has found new oil in the Atlantic off North Africa, Argentina seeks to develop shale oil in the west of its country, the Kurds in Northern Iraq hope to form a new nation financed with access to vast oil deposits, South Africa wants to turn its vast coal reserves into synthetic oil to reduce imports, Australia hopes to regain economic traction when the price of commodity resources (i.e., coal) allow it to begin profitable exporting again, Canada and its leader, Justin Trudeau, hopes to monetize the tarsands in Alberta for a more prosperous nation. Kazakhstan seeks to be the oil conduit between Europe and China. Saudi Arabia privatizes part of its behemoth Saudi Aramco to finance economic diversification, but still leaves the House of Saud firmly in power. Nigeria looks for better social harmony once oil prices rebound. It becomes all about fossil fuels. The US Permian Basin in Texas seeks new shale discoveries. Venezuela hopes to use its oil reserves to salvage its economy again once Maduro goes. Laos, Burma and Cambodia, after years of war and calamity seek exploration in their hinterlands for undiscovered oil and gas deposits. Trade deals such as the Transatlantic Trade and Investment Partnership (TTIP), United States–Mexico–Canada Free Trade Agreement (USMCA) and the Trans-Pacific Partnership (TPP) mention little if anything about climate change, and even have clauses that allow corporations to sue the governments of the host countries if laws are later passed that impact their businesses reliance on fossil fuels, such as the Canadian corporation TransCanada suing the US over rejecting the Keystone XL pipeline under then-President Barrack Obama in 2014. Hopes, dreams, economies, investments and politics of so many Westphalian nations are pinned on oil and gas, which in turn becomes the linchpin of all Westphalian finance, as we will discuss later, even named inasmuch in the form of 'sovereign bonds'. The fossil-fuel list goes on and on. Does the reader really get the picture? This is a hopeless addiction.

A GLOBAL COGNITIVE DISSONANCE, OR "SCHADENFREUDE" ENSUES

Individually, what each country is doing makes perfect economic and political sense on a very singular level. The problem is magnified when we consider these same countries in aggregate: that is, when all sovereign nations are doing it in unison. There is no collective agreement on the problem, as there can't be. Westphalia allows each state actor to merrily "do its own thing", unimpeded, to power its economy and financial activity as it sees fit under the third (and most important) principle of Westphalia *"The … non-intervention of one state in the internal affairs of another"* A strange type of cognitive dissonance has set in: Agree in Paris (and Kyoto, and Copenhagen, and Doha, and Lima, and Montreal) that the world faces an unprecedented ecological disaster with climate change and uncontrolled burning of carbon: then return to your home country and proceed as normal, without any realized outcomes until a distant 2050. Keep flying. Keep burning coal. Keep packaging in plastics. Keep driving gasoline-powered cars, trucks, buses, and motorcycles. Proceed as normal. Do not deviate. Do not restrict your exclusive, domestic right to burn fossil fuels with any binding targets that would be politically unpalatable to home constituencies. Mitigating climate change is a noble goal but can wait, we have too many pressing local issues to put this in front of our citizens anyway.

We can see that the problem is not then in addressing or acknowledging global warming and its causations, or even fixing it, the technology is there, such as for carbon sequestration, or storing the CO_2 deep in vaults underground. The root problem exists in a seventeenth-century man-made governance system that still exists as the bedrock foundation for today's Information Age nation-state, that precludes interference in any others internal affairs. Keep in mind however we are not talking about military threats or alliances against those threats, but rather climate change, which is not an acute issue, but an obtuse one. Military threats demonstrate immediate action, climate change issues, not so much.

Westphalia is accepted as normal in today's world since vested elites (as they also did in 1215 with the formulation of the Magna Carta) have too much to risk by changing it, or even venturing any radical solutions. Nonetheless, Westphalia simply does not fit neatly in today's information-intensive, data-driven, cross-border, interconnected world. Trying to justify Westphalia today, when the looming catastrophe of unmitigated fossil-fuel burning and production faces humanity cannot be overestimated. It is as serious a denial as was in denying the US institution of slavery was inherently wrong in the 1830s. Arguably, Westphalia has then become an impediment at best or threat at worst to mankind's very survival as we know it. Alarmist? No. Consider in the 2005 documentary, "*An Inconvenient Truth*", former Vice President Al Gore mistakenly believes in one of his presentations that mankind will simply "see the error of its ways" and change its behavior. He uses gold bricks on a scale on one end and earth on the other to demonstrate his point. He very wrongly assumes that the health of the planet outweighs the gold bricks. Gore got his proof theory backwards: elite interests, unfettered, and asset backed always trump collective well-wishing. It is why the rich get richer, inequality is never "corrected", and the poor continue to stay poor.

"Non-interference" also reinforces bad economic behaviors under the guise that they are benefitting the many, but actually only the few. As Naomi Klein recently put it "*self-serving individuals and actors* [elites] *undercut the potential for a[ny] collective response to the crisis*". The problem of climate change then becomes intra-systemic. "All" are waiting on the next technological marvel (inter-systemic) to solve the problem that • an invisible market hand will supposedly miraculously create. That happens where there is the defined need of a particular nation-state, or tightly shared cause, such as for building a bridge, a cross-border dam, or even a nuclear bomb. Thus a collective problem that concerns the interests of all, not a few disentangled players, can proceed immediately.

During the Cultural Revolution in China (1965–1976) under Chairman Mao ZeDong, a saying arose about ownership of public property such as parks, historical sites, nature reserves, and public commons that *"where all own, no one owns"*. Climate change is such a public goods problem where, in layspeak, no one owns it, and though it is ultimately everyone's problem, it really becomes no one's personal or individualized problem in the immediacy. Westphalia thusly allows nation-state actors to conveniently absolve themselves from any direct responsibility on the ground of economic necessity, no matter how big the fossil-fuel burning offender, be it China and India with coal, the US with oil or EU with gas.

Some economists, such as economics Nobel prize laureate William Nordhaus at Yale University, have argued that climate change then is really a "public goods" problem, which also means there is no defined entity to take direct ownership and to be held accountable. The elites especially have a strong interest in obfuscating any change that will directly affect them and their wealth. If anything, the recent Panama Papers disclosure concerning international taxation, has taught us, is that elites will go to great lengths to conceal and hide their wealth using the levers of the principle of non-interference in sovereign affairs as a cover (the World Bank and UN have been writing about this issue of elites and wealth agglomeration in Africa for years, but few have paid attention). This also gets to another issue, why do elites with resources not support the countries they are already in, such as Venezuela, Nigeria, or Malaysia, but instead patronize the financial systems of other rich countries, such as Switzerland, U.K., or the US? We will discuss this later in Chapter 9, concerning tax avoidance and transfer pricing.

If climate change is going to be dealt with successfully, the problem is systemic and structural, evolving from political will, it is not a technical problem at all, we do have the technology to solve it in the twenty-first century, such as MIT's 'Plug-and-Play' CO_2 scrubbers on existing power plants and also carbon sequestration. The root cause in this case being a centuries-old political system that allows self-absolution, indeed the exculpation, of the immediate actors. These actors being the big powers (US, Russia, UK, China, France, India, Japan, and Germany) with their economic clout and industrial policies. Change the system and you change the causation. Of course this is a tall order. The elites have so much invested in their current system of wealth and power protection within their discrete borders, that they cannot and will not change it structurally if history is any indicator of future events. This is known as the "natural state" or state of the world through human history as put forward by institutional economist and Nobel laureate Douglas North in 1990.[1]

The point to the above is that much of the liberal, multilateral crowd is placing an unassuaged faith in the strength of developed and developing country central governments. Holding them to the same standard as they would place in US or Western European governments, namely, to responsibly solve problems. This is simply misguided, and, if carried to its ultimate assumptions of acceptance, will put countries such as the US and Germany at a huge economic disadvantage in the fight against climate change while they faithfully uphold their carbon reduction pledges with strong legal institutions, but other countries do not, either by accounting perfidy, negligence, outright corruption, very weak central governance, or combination of the factors. To that end, Kyoto Protocols, Copenhagen, or Paris Accords all mean very little. So-called binding targets are not really binding on all actors, as it is a multiple-standards playing field. Western governments with high levels of institutional and transparent accountability will in fact bind themselves to these multilateral agreements at great economic costs, but developing countries with nontransparent governance, unelected officials, engineering mindsets (not legal formation), high corruption indexes, and weak institutions will fudge, if held seriously to the agreements. These are not empty statements and proof abounds. If we consider Germany with the highest retail electric prices in the world for a comparable developed country at US cents 35 per kWh, it is mostly because they have unwaveringly held up their renewable policy of Energeiwiende and other commitments (national and regional) to going green, and bestowing the costs on their citizens. Energiewiende thus is an excellent idea... if all countries did it... and their citizens could afford it... but as it stands, it is a siloed effort in Germany.[2] Despite its promise of reducing carbon, Germany is an industrial powerhouse. In 2014, it partly defaulted back to brown coal to make up for its shuttered nuclear power plants in the shadow of the Fukushima nuclear power plant disaster in March 2011.[3] Think about that: if Germany can renege.... then....

Nonetheless, other countries, such as Poland in eastern Europe, right across the border from Germany, Serbia, India, and SE Asia such as Indonesia, have simply not held up their end of the Paris commitments. They can't as their officials cannot handicap their economies. Nonetheless, CO_2 emissions do not stop at a national border, natural border, or require any visa. If countries in eastern Europe next to Germany, cannot hold up their end, what more so about dictatorships in Africa and south/central Asia where a lack of media coverage, transparency, or even competence, precludes inspection of the emissions records an accountability?

If it is then taken to its logical conclusion, the US or EU taxpayer will additionally end up subsidizing corruption in so many unrepentant nations with these agreements. Whether it be considered a wealth transfer or development assistance, this is fraught with the twin peril of waste and mismanagement. Consider that the US simply has a poor record of accounting for government largess already (i.e. Haiti, Afghanistan, Tanzania, Iraq) regarding any "development assistance", this should not be perpetuated.

Former Vice President Al Gore has said *"you can't build a 21st century economy using a 19th century blueprint"* However, Gore should step back further and consider governance under a seventeenth century Westphalian system that enshrines a framework of static sovereignty, against a twenty-first-century paradigm of mobility, analytics, and instantaneous information exchange. Westphalia by itself promotes a colonial mindset that is, from current global equality and development issues (such as the UN MDGS or "Millenium Development Goals") mitigated in its effectiveness. Correspondingly, many in the environmental movement, such as Greenpeace and the 'Fridays for Future' protest movement, have faith in big government, but big government from a Democratic rule-of-law perspective as found in the EU, Switzerland, and the US. This is simply not the same for nondemocratic countries, and cannot be dressed up as such, so a normalized baseline of governance with all actors in unison and policy simply cannot ever be assumed. Of course, supranational organizations such as IMF, World Bank, OECD, and UN draw their root power from the entire Westphalian structure, it is in their interest to promote sovereign exclusivity on an equal footing. Don't expect them to go away or disappear during any crisis, as their lifeblood and the careers of their diplomats and officers are built on world problems. This is a crucial point, who really benefits from climate change problems?

Combating Climate Change Through Derivatives

"Carbon credits" are at their core a market mechanism to keep checks and balances between carbon emitters and those mitigating carbon. It is an ethereal concept to many and needs legal certainty to be effective. Business seeks US enforcement of this eventual "carbon derivatives market" mainly to sell costly machinery and IT systems to a developing world that can ill afford it. The EU, Japan, US State of CA, and Australia have all started carbon credit markets, but are too weak to enforce them collectively outside their own legal regions, however the world runs on US dollars, if financial enforcement can be proscribed, and all countries can then be brought into the fold due to legal compliance with access to or banishment from the dollar system as the ultimate carrot and stick. We consider Argentina in 2001, Zimbabwe, and even Venezuela recently with US dollar denominated bonds, whereby starving *their own people* even becomes secondary to having access to dollars via foreign lenders.

However, even a total enforcement of carbon derivatives or carbon taxes, will still not circumvent leakage, that is countries cheating on the emissions targets, which can be considerable. Or contain mistakes, such as a damaged EXXON oil well in the US state of Ohio that leaked as much CO_2 producing methane in two weeks as some countries do in a year. The problem was only detected by satellite. What dollar enforcement will do however, is to obligate all countries to purchase US, Japanese, and EU made high-tech equipment and IT systems, and to demonstrate a sound compliance of standards processes, such as ISO or DNV. It is acknowledged however, that this equipment will not have the capacity to cut emissions inasmuch by itself, and sequester carbon. Due to corruption and poor educational systems many developing countries will not be the right venues for this type of equipment without significant retraining and cultural mindset shifts. The North–South phenomena will regurgitate and impact the developing world and population groups who will be most damaged by sea level rise, wildfires, cyclones, and deforestation. It is not by coincidence these are the South, or developing country populations in this scenario. Will China, a "South" country, lead a new carbon emissions reduction effort in lieu of an abdicated US leadership? Probably not, China has far too many domestic problems in keeping its country afloat politically to lead any international drives, additionally, Chinese companies will only really benefit via enforcement of US financial mechanisms, as their currency is inconvertible, pegged to a majority of dollars,[4] and they also, continuously, need the dollar as a medium of exchange.

Most countries are therefore still predicating their economic growth and sustenance on a continuous use of fossil fuels, thus a toothless agreement is perhaps worse than no agreement at all, as it will stand to only reinforce mal- behaviors with a politically correct smiley face that environmentalists and the general public see, but not the real underbelly of the political and financial construct, that being a noncommitment state, with perhaps even a license to emit more CO_2!

At its core then, when the veneer is stripped away, effectively combating climate change is all about involving big business, and using the levers of the US governments financial system (specifically the dollar) to ensure *legal certainties* by way of enforcement. This is the way the financial world works today, most notably in the bond markets: its all ultimately based on the US dollar. However, under a Westphalian rubric of individualized state sovereignty and insular political decisions, many which are compromised due to corruption, incompetence, insurgency or weak central governance controls, emissions leakage will not be contained. There is simply no historical precedent that all countries will suddenly come together, for "the good of the planet" or a subjective Kumbaya moment, and sacrifice their future economic growth prospects to fight an abstract lurking problem that most refuse to take ownership of anyway, or pin on Western countries as the ultimate culprit. A looming immediate problem, such as Nazi Germany perhaps, a 9.0 earthquake, or a Category Five hurricane can be a siren to action, but many cannot simply grasp the same urgency with climate change until their basement is flooded, harvest turned to dust, homestead burned down, or an out of season cyclone kills members of their own families.

Climate change is thus a politically rooted problem from the perspective in a bygone era which ensures a conditional sovereignty while ignoring the parameters of the world we live in today. Again, climate change is not a technical or financial problem. At all! We have the technology. The world also has the financial recourses. Both of these conditions are met. It is a legal application issue that cannot be applied to all nation-states equally no matter how well the intentions. Further, big business operates to the dictates of shareholders and the profit-loss (P/L) statement, not environmental conscience or well-wishing. Al Gore then was simply dead wrong in his documentary "*An Inconvenient Truth*". To ensure the value of the gold bricks in the markets requires an enforcement mechanism to uphold their ultimate retail value and protect markets that gold trades in. **This guarantor is the US legal system and its dollar ascription which underpins the entire world financial system**. No other country or region carries the same "reserve currency" status for any climate change enforcement as does the US system. Nonetheless, the US financial system is not robust enough on its own to secure the leakage or mistake issue as discussed. It will have to rely on the information and data provided by (usually compromised) foreign central governments. But again, that can be largely controlled for by established standards, whereby effectiveness is verified for compliance by empowered monitors. Additionally, we now have the tools for real time enforcement and data collection: 5G and the blockchain. The fifth generation (5G) of telecommunications ensures almost seamless transmission of data, whereas the blockchain can store vast quantities of data, from inception to current disposition of any construct that can be digitalized. Data storage that cannot be altered or changed for political needs. In short, the technology exists today.

Nonetheless, what is good for the markets is not always good for the citizens! Enforcement will carry a high price tag that US and other Western developed country taxpayers will be forced to bear for the rest of world (and in particular the equipment/technology vendors!) for their being a definitive "court of last resort". As we've seen before, a system of privatizing the profits for US\EU companies and their technology transfers to the developing world must be ensured firstly, while socializing the enforcement mechanisms costs to all. Business wants mandated enforceable carbon targets through US dollar revenues, not so much is their concern about future generations but rather about ensuring a new revenue stream under an open "Blue Market" of climate change. What we are saying here is that nothing will be regulated or enacted unless financial elites and their holdings are part of the solution. They simply cannot be excluded, it is the historical natural order.

Spectrum of Values... and Very Unbalanced

Consider that abolishing the institution of slavery in the US took a civil war. The fall of the Soviet Union took many years and was marked by a nuclear arms race followed by an economic collapse. The Roman Empire disintegrated over four centuries, the Ottoman Empire even longer. The world simply does not have the luxury of time however to address a climate change issue over the centuries, though the abstract ethereality of it may present that illusion, and falsely create a sense of ambiguity. The Westphalian system cannot be defaulted to as an *"only way of life"*, it must be confronted and soon. Simply, the same level of thinking that created the Westphalian system in 1648 cannot be the thinking used to absolve the modern nation-state in the twenty-first century of its global responsibility, namely planetary stewardship, not *mea culpa's* and economic activity first, however odd this may seem, or however entrenched the actors.

As mentioned in Chapter 1, cultural values in different places also influence standards and outcomes. And getting to one common standard, that is enforceable across all countries and regions is the real problem. The assumption is that all nations will report and tackle climate change as equals. But the cracks have been showing for several years. African nations demand payments to change their systems, but with long histories of corrupt governments, many doubt the funds from rich countries will ever be used for that. Asian countries like China and India, want more time to pollute to stabilize their economic growth initiatives before committing to any fossil-fuel cutbacks. Excuses abound.

Western countries and their territories have different levels of standards to mitigate carbon: Australia, Germany, and the US state of CA all have carbon trading markets, but with different standards. None of these standards have been harmonized, and none can really agree on a "price for carbon", meaning what price should per ton of carbon should heavily polluting companies actually pay? $10? $50? $100? Noting that whatever price is agreed on, costs will ultimately be passed on to consumers in their respective Westphalian states. So it becomes a politically sensitive discussion and highly contentious. As before mentioned, Germans are reeling under the highest electricity costs in Europe, whereas Chinese enjoy some of the cheapest electricity, with their overabundance of capacity due to a plethora of coal-fired plants, that ironically, Germany has been trying to phase out! Additionally, some developing countries such as Ecuador, Nigeria, Mexico or Egypt, subsidize fossil fuels to keep their poverty-stricken economies moving. We can see that without uniformity in CO_2 emissions enforcement, there are too many cross purposes and it becomes a zero-sum game. Since Westphalia promotes exclusivity, uniformly enforced standards across nations are suspect to manipulation and meddling, and of course, always the ever-growing nationalist cry against any form of "one-world governance" or "foreign interference" continuously ensues. We should also consider that uniformly agreed standards must be in place to measure how carbon emissions are calculated. Some nations in EU have very robust measurement systems, others, such as India, have leakage that can be exacerbated more by bribes and corrupt officials. Consider that the corruption in India is so bad that the leader in November 2016, Narendra Modi, demonetized 90% of the value of all circulating paper currency, to flush out illegal money. The results were weak, but the national pandemonium caused was great, the leader at least received accolades for trying to "do something" about India's incipient corruption.

In the information age, this entire nation-state debate needs a reformatting and reframing. The solution here then is that solving the challenge of climate change is not found in technical advancement or assessing financial responsibility to a pool of ever shirking actors, but rather in a systems analysis with a cross-border response to this issue as a feedbacking mechanism. In this sense we are using a customized approach, instead of a one-size-fits-all approach, namely, a world "carbon price", that everyone is supposed to agree on, and enforced with a dollarized ascription as we will suggest in Chapter 10. Without any real enforcement entity, ongoing debate or accords are useless.

Nonetheless, could climate change still be solved under Westphalia if the issues of socio-economics alone are addressed? It is a good question. Possible, though extremely remote. World nations have only really come together to solve disastrous, looming problems, such as WW II, when a pending Fascist doom was atop all of them. Climate change is a lurking problem, not an immediate threat, as most will not feel its extreme consequences in this lifetime even, thus the urgency to act quickly wanes, especially diminished as news of cold fronts or blizzards hit the US or EU, which are the drivers of the developed world's media outlets. It will be subsequent generations that are a century down the line that will feel its worst effects.

Worrying about future generations makes for great headlines, but is rarely digested in the here and now world we face. Further, coalescing nations to fight a lurking threat requires strict control of information, usually by elite actors, and through *their* interpretation only of the threat. Today's world of instantaneous information would seemingly mute that, thus instead of controlling information, Westphalian elites have a very vested "here and now" interest in garbling the interpretation by presenting as many viewpoints, scientific and unscientific, as possible; i.e., constantly presenting climate change as "unsettled or disputed" science, on a very long impact timeline, and giving equal weight to other theories of there being no real deviance in historic temperatures. While misguided, this is the media reality we have in the digital age.

The entire notion then of seeking to get nation-states to collectively "do something" together on their own altruistic accord about climate change is the wrong approach. Climate change is not about people not "wanting to do their part". It is not an atomized issue that can be confronted that simplistically. That thinking will doom any grand initiative as it will always depend on another actor going first (i.e., the public goods dilemma, or some may say the "Spanish Prisoner" situation) to solve the issue. The realization needs to be directed at changing the seventeenth-century system that the world is so hopelessly locked into already deep into the twenty-first century! Identifying and overcoming this systemic problem is the first step in being able to seriously confront any planetary threat, not worrying about all the semantical niceties and nuances of keeping it going. We simply cannot objectively address a major environmental catastrophe of twenty-first-century climate change with a political-economic construct created by seventeenth-century elitism for seventeenth-century elites within their very confined borders, and limited knowledge of the non-European world.

VOLUNTARY EFFORTS?

There is much enthusiasm among the younger generations for voluntary climate reduction efforts. Such as paying extra for a plane ticket, banning plastic straws, reusing plastic bags, not washing towels during a stay in a hotel, owning a Tesla, or buying carbon credits with merchandise purchases on a "Green" credit card. Due to a lack of enforcement and oversight standards, there is no telling if the money, or savings, from these activities really does limit or go into climate mitigation or into another fund. In short, voluntary public actions are just like Westphalian nations: only as strong as the weakest link. Further, these voluntary efforts don't get to the major polluting roots of the problem: gigantic coal-fired power plants in India and China, monstrous traffic jams in Jakarta, LA, or Bangkok, massive and growing banks of electric consuming air conditioners in the MENA, thousands of daily fossil fueled commuter flights in the EU, diesel fueled super-cargo ships traversing the Pacific Ocean to the US. Individualized climate reduction efforts are only a very token effort at best, and no, not everyone is doing their part. There is no "feel good" ending of hope and change for this chapter. Climate change is what it is, and is hamstrung by a confluence of political issues and the people involved who have little, if any, initiative to change their behaviors without serious consequences. This is the crux of the matter, and the theme throughout this book.

POSTSCRIPT: PLASTIC WASTE

Recently, a new cross-border problem has emerged that has gotten significant media traction: plastic waste. Similar to climate change this is also a public goods dilemma that no one country wants to own. Plastic trash, like CO_2 is also produced by crude oil and natural gas. It has very long physical attributes, and can take up to 800 years to break down. It now litters the oceans and land on an enormous scale. In time, with sun and seawater it breaks down into smaller, molecularized components, but the molecules remain intact, to be eaten by smaller animals, moving up the food chain as they are in turn eaten by larger predators, and ultimately by humans. Large swaths of plastic waste circulate in the oceans, some covering vast areas as big as the US state of Texas. The long-term health effects of this are still unknown, but the science regarding the chain of plastic movement is all there. Again, this problem is not technical either. It is political, tucked deep inside the Westphalian system. It is simply cheaper to use plastic as opposed to wood, or other material derivatives. As we shall see, a monetized value placed also on plastic, and enforced will go a long way to undermining Westphalian norms of inaction. See more stories and issues to arise in the media the next few years about this problem, along with the same tired Westphalian framework of protocols and accords seeking to address it, attendant with no coherent results. The world runs on fossil fuels, not only for transportation, but also for the cheap plastic the world depends on for modern life.

Notes

1. Late institutional economist and Nobel Laureate Douglass North has written extensively about human order and elite control of societies throughout history.
2. Schiermeier, Q. (10 April 2013). Renewable Power: Germany's Energy Gamble: An Ambitious Plan to Slash Greenhouse-Gas Emissions Must Clear Some High Technical and Economic Hurdles. Nature. https://doi.org/10.1038/496156a. Retrieved on May 1, 2016.
3. Andresen, T. (15 April 2014). Coal Returns to German Utilities Replacing Lost Nuclear. Bloomberg. Retrieved on February 19, 2019.
4. As will be discussed in Chapter 6 about financial markets, the US dollar is really the only game in town and China, the world's biggest carbon emissions polluter, pegs its currency to a 'basket of currency' of which the majority holding (>60%) are in dollars.

Bibliography

Andresen, Tino. (15 April 2014) *Coal Returns to German Utilities Replacing Lost Nuclear*. Bloomberg. Retrieved on February 19, 2019.

Brewer, R. G. (2019) *We Cant Stop Drilling for Oil, BP Says....* The Motley Fool. http://finance.yahoo.com/news/apos-t-stop-drilling-oil-221600736.html. Retrieved on April 9, 2019.

Chang, J. (2006) *Mao: The Unknown Story*. Vintage Books.

Ford Record Sales. http://www.ft.com/cms/s/0/975d45f8-0d37-11e6-ad80-67655613c2d6.html. Retrieved on November 2017.

Gore, A. (2005) An Inconvenient Truth. Documentary.

Klein, N. (2014) *This Changes Everything*. London: Allen Lane.

McKibben, W. (2012) Global Warming's Terrifying New Math. *Rolling Stone Magazine*. http://www.rollingstone.com/politics/news/global-warmings-terrifying-new-math-20120719. Retrieved on July 7, 2017.

Nordhaus, W. (2005) *Paul Samuelson and Global Public Goods*. Yale University Essay, 5/5.

Schiermeier, Quirin. (10 April 2013) Renewable Power: Germany's Energy Gamble: An Ambitious Plan to Slash Greenhouse-Gas Emissions Must Clear Some

High Technical and Economic Hurdles. *Nature*. https://doi.org/10.1038/496156a. Retrieved on May 1, 2016.

http://www.madamasr.com/contributor-profile/moritz-mihatsch. Retrieved on November 2017.

http://www.articlemyriad.com/relevance-westphalian-system-modern-world-sasha-safonova/. Retrieved on October 2017.

http://thinkprogress.org/climate/2016/05/02/3774418/ttip-greenpeace-leaks/. Retrieved on November 2017.

CHAPTER 3

Universal Basic Income: Populism Comes to the Fore

In his May 2017 graduation speech at Harvard University, Facebook founder and CEO Mark Zuckerberg called vigorously for governments to pay all their citizens a living wage or "Universal Basic Income",[1] also known as a UBI. Bill Gates the founder of Microsoft, has also supported this, as has Tesla CEO Elan Musk. The concept plays well before any audience in an age of underemployment, with the high costs of education, and low job mobility in part due to spiraling domestic costs, that keep people locked in their place. Currently, the UBI is one of the most hotly debated policy topics to address income inequality worldwide. Before the concept of a UBI is brushed off as merely some overpaid CEO's ideological world view of what "should be" from a high-level C-Suite, it should be considered that populism worldwide has been driving some distorted outcomes from traditional political thinking recently: Brexit, Trump, the Five-Star movement in Italy, to consider a few. Further, the recent election of US New York representative Alexandria Ocasio-Cortez with a green "New Deal" has no doubt also put this issue in the crosshairs.[2] Politically then, a UBI may not be as distant a concept as it seems to be.

With exploding world populations, increased wealth inequality and rising disparity, research into artificial intelligence (AI), and the automation of jobs, such as driverless taxi's, trucks, drones, and fully robotized assembly lines,[3] the utopian idea of promoting a workless society, with all sharing equally in the revenues, has reemerged and been given a new life. Whether history rhymes or repeats, this is essentially the crypto-concept of Karl Marx and his 1848 *Communist Manifesto*: providing an egalitarian

© The Author(s) 2020
W. Hickey, *The Sovereignty Game*,
https://doi.org/10.1007/978-981-15-1888-1_3

and decent standard of living for all the proletariat from the productive capacity of wealth-hoarding entitled classes, like Zuckerberg, Jeff Bezos, and Bill Gates. In other words, class struggle, which is being perpetuated in today's[4] populist era is still alive and well. The late sociologist and Marxist scholar, Erik Olin Wright, had been pushing for a UBI for many years, based on the concept of an egalitarian future alternative to capitalism.[5]

Communism by now has been thoroughly discredited as a legitimate form of governance. It's high ideals, similar to a UBI, are simply not how they played out when juxtaposed against human greed, self-interest, and motivation. The twain could not meet. All that communism ultimately delivered was to form a new class of entitled, insulated leaders accountable only to themselves, but is this any different than any governmental authority with power, as the writer Ayn Rand would coalesce them together. The politics and enlarged bureaucracy behind any proposed UBI would essentially do the same: create just another giant government bureaucracy in itself to administer it. While new technology like the blockchain could essentially allow it to be a peer-to-peer (P2P) administrative format, elite interests could not allow it to be a simple, untested, cash transfer to all. It would allow rent-seeking officials to have a say in the matter. Big bureaucracy would become an ingrained and costly administrative part of any UBI initiative.[6] Large government programs attract many empty hands.

As worldwide inequality grows, under pressure politicians feel they must "do something" to correct the inequality imbalance. This requires hard political choices, but they want a default, to a baseline of orthodox economic models and forecasts that tell them "all will be well" if they implement this or that untried economic plan. The problem is that most economic modeling is bankrupt[7] in this age, change is happening too quickly for any economic models to respond and social media spreads information, that becomes distorted and difficult to track in real time. Nonetheless, a UBI is proposed as an antidote to a worst-case scenario of increasing income inequality, where rapid technological advances significantly displace human employment, lead to an increase in said income inequality, a continued hollowing out of the middle-class, and even riots, social unrest, with the attendant creation of a permanent, unemployable "underclass".

Theoretically today, any job that carries repetitive manual tasks can be done by a robot[8] at the least, or a fully automated process at the best. As the creep of AI moves up the ladder of skills, it begins to replace higher paying jobs that are not only based on repetitive tasking, but also decision-making. It would seem then that the biggest future threat to middle-class workers in developed countries is not losing their jobs to developing ones, but rather automation, in both developed and developing countries.[9] This is of course not new thinking, and was amplified 20 years ago with the work of Lester Thurow at MIT predicting "tectonic workplace shifts" in a new economy, and Jeremy Rifkin lamenting in, "*The End of Work*" about a robotized, automated world[10] leaving everyone without jobs. However, *Polyani's Paradox* suggests differently, which is about tacit knowledge that a map, a book, or a computer program simply cannot decipher. "We know more than we can tell", for example, a local taxi driver in any country, developed or developing, will have much better tacit (or gut level) knowledge of the area than any "Google Maps" application provided to a new driver, or even a machine-driven car.[11] Google Maps however, has not put taxi drivers out of business, but Uber has instead created more competition for them[12] by shifting the capacity paradigm from a few licensed taxi drivers to a DIY taxi driver job creation. Many jobs require uniquely human characteristics such as empathy, creativity, judgment, or critical thinking—and that jobs of this nature can never succumb to widespread automation.[13] In this sense, we may need well to focus on the softer aspects of jobs as opposed to simply data analysis and calculations to automate everything.

Customization Versus Modularization

Car manufacturing, drilling for oil, making washing machines, sorting coffee beans, cleaning carpets, packaging instant noodles, assembling iPhones, etc. All of these processes can remove the human factor with robotization. However, robots cannot customize, quickly change course, or make fine subjective comparisons in products (shoe leather quality) and services (cleaning behind the curtain, under the Lazyboy, or on top of the refrigerator), areas that are still "technologically lagging".[14] Besides the taxi driver, consider some other simple examples, of automated versus customized jobs.

Job type	Automated (modular)	Customization (maintenance)
Transport	Driverless cars	UBER
Sorting	Amazon.com (dispatching)	Amazon.com (pickers)
Banking	ATM	Relationship banking
Automotive assembly	Assembly line first production	After-market accessories
Lawncare	Robotized Yazoo lawnmower	Hand trimming a putting green

Source David Autor, MIT Economist as adapted by Will Hickey

The point with this is that the human factor is still there and much needed, and some may argue growing, not receding with customization drives amidst a sea of automated standardization and modularization. An issue in the oil and automotive business for example is that for insurance to payout claims, parts and equipment, such as pipelines in a refinery or gasoline to natural gas conversion for a car motor, must be "replaced as new" or a modular replacement, as opposed to any refurbishment, repair, or customization. It becomes then a CAPEX (capital expenditures) versus OPEX (operational expenditures) accounting issue. This is an extremely important nuance as it gets to the crux of job creation versus total automation, in other words, are the laws and policies we have preventing real craftsmanship? A craftsmanship that requires lifelong vocational skills and committed training?

Financial management has made capital expenses more easily obtainable than additional operation expenses, thereby allowing the introduction of mal-incentives into the organization. By this we mean, it is more readily accepted to replace things than to pay for the labor to fix them. These financial policies thus encourage a deferment of costs instead of active maintenance of existing objects. Consider the entire tax investigation of US equipment giant Caterpillar in April 2017, where an offshore (Swiss) company was formed, not for creation of any product, but simply to conduct sales accounting for an agglomeration of profits selling new parts to developing countries. It has been so successful, that Caterpillar is lauded as having two revenue streams one for new equipment, the other for selling Western priced parts and services into perpetuity in developing countries, namely Africa, which has commodity-driven economies and high domestic unemployment. In other words, *high-cost*, automation-driven modularity, not any *low-cost* local refurbishment of that equipment, which could provide scores of vocational jobs, is the entire business model rule.[15] Automation forced by a Western business process that minimizes any local labor differential usage or development of that local labor component.

This leads us to an implication that is almost exclusively for financial management, namely, that policy drives financially unsound long-term decisions. In short, it becomes a piece of compelling evidence that it is always cheaper to keep the asset maintained and repaired (manpower) than it is to try replace it (automation) without further vocational or maintenance craftsmanship, or interference, involved.[16]

One avenue here then is that instead of a UBI, poly-technical skills and repair be reintroduced into processes and systems that have become static and costly due to these regulations or warranties. In essence, litigation that has stymied jobs creation. Simply put, costly modular replacement has become the norm of the future, rewarding business owners and shareholders, but sidelining mechanics and maintenance workers with the chance to grow, learn, practice, and exercise their skills on a transactional level, namely for creating value. We need value creation through people, that being craftsmanship, where in many developing countries, the labor cost differential alone will be much cheaper than buying new components. Simply, people need to work, to take pride in their work, not be given handouts.

Substance of a UBI

Again, we are not simply rehashing the effects of automation replacing jobs. So much has been written about this already, and the double whammy of AI replacing know-how jobs is now in-hand with automated process, such as self-driving cars, and drones. Rather this discussion is about the salary replacement component to masse redundancy via automation and robotization. The core of the UBI proposal is that of a cash transfers to all affected, who will really pay, and how it effects motivations. A core pillar of the UBI is it will "free up" people to pursue other activities by ensuring an economic safety net. But that is half-baked, as it does not consider knock-on effects of mitigated learning and lost skills due to atrophy or disuse.

In its simplest form, a UBI is a non-means tested cash transfer to those made obsolete (or redundant) by technology accumulation in the labor market, with the acknowledged fact they will neither be able to be employed again soon, nor gain the appropriate technical commercial skills (i.e., welding, operating a lathe, programming code, etc.) necessary to engage on a productive level in the workforce. As stated, automation can create many specialty custom jobs in itself,[17] but unemployed construction welders over 40 are simply not going to learn software IT programming quickly. The idea behind the UBI is that due to their current dispositions, and the fact the world is growing more costly for everyone, they should be "compensated" in short order by the advanced society at large.

Whether a UBI would be means tested or not (some making above a certain income would not be eligible for it such as in Finland or Canada)[18] in the future is a parallel discussion. While means testing would seem in order, direct transfers to the "rest of society", would breed class resentment and create a demotivated workforce. Further, the French sociologist, Michel Crozier, never underestimated people's ability to game systems for deriving a continuous personal benefit from the bureaucracy within which they exist.[19] This is a profound understanding of human nature in modern systems that should not be lost. Any successful UBI initiative would have to target those really in need, but this is not the utopian view expressed by Silicon Valley executives or certain wealthy countries. Perhaps one could take a lesson from Singapore or Saudi Arabia when considering paying people for not doing anything: their citizens then refuse to do any manual labor, and all real labor has to be imported from other, poorer countries. This again is linked to the cross-border issue of paying people based on their passport, not their skills (Chapter 4) and represents a serious leakage in the Westphalian system in our data-driven world.

The next logical question would be where would the payment for a UBI come from? The government (who will derive it from taxes on society), the owners of the businesses (who will pass the costs on to customers), or a tax on the robots and the machinery themselves (which will also pass the costs on to consumers). Of course there is no free lunch. Ultimately, a UBI will effectively become a societal gainsharing tax device. All will have to pay an effective tangible cost for enjoying technological upgrades under any UBI scheme, similar to a GST or VAT. In short then, it appears any UBI would be considered as a wealth transfer mechanism.

Why a UBI Is so Problematic

A UBI, promoted on its website http://basicincome.org sends a strong message that you will be compensated for just being wonderful you. One needs not to make effort to adapt to technology, to try harder, to learn more, to take risks, or to create any value-added transactional activity on their own, they can just reap the benefits by sitting on their hands. An entitlement mindset creeps in. Yet, world demographics and stagnant economic growth has long ago shown us that this is an untenable position in many countries. Most economies are simply not strong enough to administer any robust application of a UBI. It has a real, not hidden, cost that is similar to any large government program or expanded bureaucracy.

An article in the *Atlantic Magazine* in 2015 wrote misleadingly that welfare made people more entrepreneurial. To be precise, entrepreneurs did in fact do better when certain welfare benefits such as food stamps, were available, but welfare in itself, did not create entrepreneurs. Even though many entrepreneurs did not apply for the benefits, just knowing that that financial backstop was there encouraged them to take more risks, and not fear any financial ruin which is also a key argument of the Gates/Musk/Zuckerberg/Ellison high-tech crowd. This is just a few cases though, overall, bigger government programs do not create entrepreneurs, and further, most people are simply not cut out to be risk-taking entrepreneurs.[20] They seek a structured job format and being told exactly what to do. But we don't live in that world anymore. With or without a UBI, everyone is forced to become a risk taker.

Simply speaking we do not know how people will react long-term with regard to work incentives and productivity with UBI in place instead of a wage level that is more or less related to their performance. It is a big gamble to introduce this with so little evidence about its economic impact. One need look no further than American Indians on reservations or Aboriginal tribes in Australia (or even consider big jackpot lottery winners) to see the immediate effects of non-means tested cash payouts to large identity groups: Drug addiction, shortened life spans, under-education, family violence, and poverty soar, not to mention unemployment, the same issue the UBI is reflexively trying to circumvent! Yet in this case, the medicine of a UBI may cause more illness.

In the long run, perhaps over 50 years from now, technology, robots, automation, etc., may have taken us to a stage where this kind of thinking is irrelevant. People may not need to "work" as in our current lexicon. Today, most of our basic needs do in fact flow from computer steered production systems. But that does not mean that we will not need to work. Work may be redefined and seen in another context, or perhaps a new definition. The basic fact that you must contribute to share in the rewards will still be there, and hard workers will always be sought out and rewarded. In this aspect, perhaps a new definition of work, linking one's overall contribution, or aggregated transactional activity, to society directly as opposed to one's contribution to an abstract gross national product (GNP) is in order.[21]

Many do not believe in this kind of egalitarianism. While grievances against inequality are on the rise, and warranted by the hideous *"race to the bottom"* development we have seen recently in many autocratic developing countries, but yet, it does not yet seem to be a way to move forward.

A UBI Is Misguided

Again, a major argument in favor of a "cash transfer" program or UBI is that by having an economic safety net in place, particularly in a high-cost area such as San Francisco or Paris, local people would be encouraged to assume greater economic risks, namely entrepreneurial, in their activities.[22] Yet, a UBI is a political contrivance designed to deflect attention from real issues in society: restructuring initiatives that can create endogenous growth activity in countries. In other words societies are failing to fully engage and embrace the information age, choosing instead to rely on old paradigms of work, and bailing out old industry, usually enshrined in the state-owned enterprises (SOE). They are not addressing how to put people to work but rather, how to bulwark select groups, such as taxi drivers, factory workers, hotel operators, longshoremen, and plumbers from competition and change. In this sense, a UBI becomes a political artifice, not a remedy for societal or uncompetitive ills. This is the crux of the argument.

Here is the problem: As Einstein said, we simply cannot solve today's problems at the same level of thinking that created them. This is not to say we are suggesting a new answer, but that a UBI is clearly not thought out, it is half-baked and populist, and anything that attempts to minimize human transactions, or the human interface, to create value with an overall technological manifestation is simply misguided. Humanity exists and thrives on the creation and propagation of individualized transactions. Work is enshrined as a crucial part of mankind's existence, psychology, and historical identity, his very DNA.

People Supporting a UBI Are More Misguided

The idyllic experience of poet David Thoreau taking to the woods dreaming of an existence free of traditional obligations, is simply that, a utopian ideal at best. A UBI will not create that paradigm, where a world of robots and automatic assembly lines free humankind from any transactional responsibility. Nonetheless, Musk,[23] Zuckerberg, Thomas Piketty, and Dambisa Moyo[24] and most recently US Vermont representative Bernie Sanders, have promoted this idea, perhaps as a type of VIP endorsement of the inequality issue with increased automation, that some of them also have a direct stake in, it is a conduit for populist backlash. However, while socially popular, it is also reactionary, and a circular thinking: automation puts people out of work, some entity must be held responsible, people out of work must be made whole by that entity, meaning the entity (automation) that puts people out of work must be held responsible, etc.

Further, governments have now begun espousing the idea, notably Switzerland, (a rich country with a tiny population), Mexico,[25] Finland, Canada, and India, (a mega-country with a huge, impoverished population). A UBI is something Switzerland might possibly afford being the world's richest per capita banking capital, but is definitely not something India can afford with a per capita gross domestic product (GDP) of around $1500 a year. There are some reasons for this that will be expressed further.

Two Examples of a "Near UBI": Indonesia and Alaska

The comparables to a UBI are nonexistent, however, examples of institutional plans for cash transfers can be deduced, as there are some developing countries that have tried them.[26] Again, it is important to caution these are not the same as a UBI, they target specific groups (children, mothers, elderly), are conditional (such as in certain remote provinces), and are only in developing countries. Further they are all very small sums of money, certainly nothing nearly as grandiose as the CHF 2500 Swiss government proposed UBI, which was soundly defeated by voters in 2016.[27] We note, again, that a non-means tested UBI is being proposed for all in developed as well as developing countries.

Country	Program name	Targeted group	Effect
Brasil	Bolsa Escolar	School children	Overall positive
Indonesia	Various, BLT and PKH	Children, mothers, destitute	Mixed effectiveness
Mexico	Prospera	Impoverished families	Overall positive
Philippines	Pantawid Pamilyang[28]	Children's health/education	Selectively effective
South Africa	Social pension[29]	Elderly	Very new, unknown

Indonesia, for example, tried targeted cash transfer programs (*Program Jaring Pengaman Sosial*) to its impoverished areas after the first economic crisis of 1998 crippled its economy. While initiating some changes for the better, mortality rates dropped, and school enrollments increased, they also left out large sections of the rural poor population which did not have identification or could verify their poverty status. Stronger institutions needed to be in place for its administration as beneficiary selection becomes contentious and problematic. Some poor in wealthy regions received it, yet some very poor in desolate areas didn't, suggesting bureaucrats and connections with them are a determinant. The findings of the Indonesia cash transfer program suggest they needed to have both a long-term view of the the programs themselves, as well as a short-term, formative evaluation to assess their immediate impacts, and change course if necessary.[30]

Another paradigm for UBI consideration, is not a simple cash transfer at all, but a natural resource sharing plan, as found with the US State of Alaska's "*Permanent Fund*". Unlike conditional cash transfers, this is not means or identity tested, but freely available to all citizens of that state. Due to the "resource curse" and "looting of resources" (where those in power take and appropriate the resources for themselves, not the community) it would be difficult to find a comparable program in a developing country. The important qualifier here is that it is a democratic sharing plan for *all residents* based on profits realized from Alaska oil and mining revenues, meaning Alaska has the actual physical resources to pay for this plan, not intangible ones. A benefit of roughly $1000 a year,[31] free of any means testing, is paid directly to every citizen in the state of Alaska. No work is required. Yet, and this is important, Alaska is the most violent state in the US, with also the highest unemployment rate[32] and the highest rate of illicit drug use among people under 25. Apparently,

Alaska's cash transfer program has not alleviated deep social ills, and it is quite possible it has even exacerbated them.[33]

One thing that does stand out in all cash transfer and national resource sharing plans is a jobs creation program for newly minted government bureaucrats to verify, administer, account for, and evaluate all the recipients. Even for non-means tested, a financial transfer mechanism must be put in place to administer and verify all of the payments. Bureaucracy grows. Nonetheless, the blockchain, the technology underpinning Bitcoin, has some promise in facilitation of direct payments without the need of any intermediary, be it bank, or government.

A UBI Is Already Technically in Place: Unstructured State-Owned Companies

If another "de facto reality" is considered, we already have a UBI in place: the many Federal and State jobs (and in particular, giant state-owned company jobs, such as in China, India, Brazil, or Indonesia, where redundancy and nonproductive work, such as collecting or "pushing paper" for no tangible value-added activity, still thrive). Many of these are simply nonproductive jobs, usually politically driven in nature, with career employees, who while well meaning, cannot be fired, as long at they show up for work. If we are basing analysis based on efficiency and value creation, these jobs would in its most broadest definition possibly themselves qualify as a UBI.

A developing world that relies far too much on low value "exports" as opposed to restructuring their economies to promote endogenous growth activity, like Korea, Taiwan, or Singapore have done via value-added activity and higher quality products is another problem. Many so-called "export dependent economies" such as China, Vietnam, and Indonesia exist by utilizing the low hanging fruit of cheap labor in the former and raw commodities in the latter two. Nonetheless, higher cost labor is now hurting China as it grows into a middle income economy, bureaucracy as always, stymying Vietnam, and depressed commodity prices humbling Indonesia. Yet it is the fixation with their export-oriented economic models that is problematic. Even if they do develop further, many have a tendency to get mired in the so-called "Middle Income Trap", namely, they reach a state of comfort with their exports and fail to innovate or diversify economically further and with rising labor costs, lose their competitive edge with what products they do export.[34]

Resentment Factors

All politically correct semantics aside, the age of large families to satisfy a cultural, religious, or ethnic prerogative is simply no longer sustainable on a planet with now 7.2 plus billion people.[35] We consider that subsidizing large families with a UBI would be to penalizing those who have exercised fiscal and social responsibility with childbearing on an overcrowded planet, such as in Korea, Japan, or Norway, countries now with negative population growth. Nonetheless, many cultures in equatorial Africa, India, Indonesia, South Asia, Latin America, and the Middle East continue to have more children than they or their societies can ever economically support on a Western standard in an increasingly costly, and dollar ascripted world. China should be considered the anomaly here, years of its totalitarian 'one-child' policy have served to depress the population. Nonetheless, despite scrapping the policy in 2016, many are still choosing to have only one child due to rising costs.

This issue may be even more problematic in implementing a UBI where traditionally racially homogenous, and smaller families, such as in Sweden or Australia, are now assimilating large migrant populations with cultures where inter-ethnicity and large families are the rule, such as Nigerians, Arabs, or Indians, and whereby these countries also exhibit diverse ethnicities and beliefs (Islam, Buddhism, Hinduism, etc.) not typically found in their new host locales. Namely, is it the responsibility of citizens in those countries to bear the costs of different cultures for assimilation, when those different cultures to not recognize the same cost and obligations required. This is a problem with the Westphalia system, and also in promoting a UBI: that is, who ultimately pays economically and socially for cross-border impacts?

The "Break-Even" of Labor Costs Versus Automation

A UBI could also quite possibly exacerbate a race to the bottom scenario, whereby countries without it exploit cut rate human labor via poor conditions and safety at the expense of costly, automated machinery. This is not hyperbole: if companies can marginally save on the costs of expensive automated equipment by defaulting to cheaper human labor, they will.

This dehumanization of the workforce thereby cuts two ways: automation that negates human interface, and creates slavery *de ja vu*, where autocratic countries with a need for any foreign investment and without labor rights, "pimp out" their people to the lowest common denominator as an offset to countries with a costly UBI in place. Candidate countries for this would be Cambodia, Laos, Sudan, North Korea, and Myanmar, countries with very weak human rights records, and dictatorial political regimes. Again, Westphalia dictates economic exclusivity, not economic cooperation, beggar they neighbor policies flow and prevail from this construct, where the chips will land, no one knows.

MOTIVATIONAL STUDIES AND WORK

Social Scientist Elton Mayo's *Hawthorne Effect'* from the 1930s' human performance studies at *Western Electric* in Cicero, IL, taught us that people take pride in being observed by others in doing their work and being engaged. With a UBI there is no engagement, there is no doing. It is a political payola that panders to certain economic groups if not means tested, and even if means tested, only perpetuates the welfare state. Perhaps an underlying issue with a UBI then is not so much income as recognition in an era of hypermedia, mass production, and social networks. Everyone seeks appreciation. As Elton Mayo discovered, paying attention to human needs increases their productivity.[36] Later Abraham Maslow and Frederick Hertzberg considered needs and workplace factors as drivers in motivation. Yet, recent human resources theory has shown that simply being happy or more efficient does not ensure added productivity or better initiative.[37]

Psychologically then, most human beings seek to be "in demand" and feel that they want to do something useful. Intrinsically, many people do not wish to be paid for doing nothing. They need the money to survive, but also seek appreciation for their efforts. A UBI cuts that link of self-worth. It might easily lead to human beings floating around without self-respect and self-esteem, a psychologically and socially damaging detrimental aspect of the UBI. Many of us compare our wages to what we do and what other people get—as a standard of self-actualization. People intrinsically feel the need for some kind of fairness, and do not mind if the well-compensated CEO of a company or professional footballer gets much more, but we certainly do mind if we feel that somebody is overcompensated compared to what "I get" measured against our relative performance. People should not be rewarded for simply failing to adapt to change, as when things change they may not simply grasp their full significance.[38] Simply put, a UBI may temper this inclination. For a UBI to be effective, it would need to motivate as opposed to simply placate recipients. Otherwise, just another government welfare program is created, where cash transfers are a direct subsidy and have an especially high risk of undermining the individual's self-esteem and self-reliance.[39]

What Happens Next?

Right now a UBI is just a concept, driven by populist angst against the rise in automation that until recently has killed blue-collar manufacturing jobs, but which now threatens white-collar office and technical jobs, worldwide. As a UBI grows in world appeal especially with media seeking Silicon Valley titans championing it, and populist mass movements such as in Switzerland and even India, responsible forces in favor of individual productivity and entrepreneurism must have counter arguments against this trend.[40] Left by itself, a UBI is a suspect concept that at the least will promote world disharmony by playing on competitive labor advantages of poor countries and at the worst, class warfare due to perceptions of "wealth transfer" and beneficiary selection that promotes more inequality. Again, we hearken back to the fact that in human society, only transactions can create value, this is the foundation of all economic cycles.[41]

A good research question to ask then might be "Does a UBI create more entrepreneurial activity and business dynamism?" This is unknown and unknowable, as no comparables exist. It could promote entrepreneurial activity for *a few* people by giving them a safety net. The biggest problem with any UBI will be unintended economic consequences that give way to mal-economic activities (goldbricking) or distorted outcomes (such as pay for "non-performance"), at this point, human ingenuity has always derived a way to game systems[42] in particular, heavily bureaucratic ones. On an international level, and under a Westphalian framework, it will increase "beggar thy neighbor" tendencies with serious implications. For example, countries with robust automation and a UBI, such as Korea or Finland, will be played off against "slave labor" conditions of Laos or Bangladesh, where the result will be a "marginal comparative advantage" cost outcome. It's all about costs anyway, so its clear where capital will flow.

The twenty-first-century is the information age. Everything we do and use from starting the car, to ordering at a restaurant, to banking, to shopping for shoes, to turning on the cell phone, is bolstered by technology somehow. Automation will have a negative effect on low-skilled workers the next generation, but research has shown it will have *drastic effects* for the middle-skilled employees, such as technicians and supervisors. Skills in an automated world for computer coding, and IT simply cannot be learned overnight, but must be built on. Most people do not possess the ability nor the motivation to relearn these types of skills, especially as they age they are even less inclined to do so.[43] Universities, political bastions as they are, still refuse to adapt swaths of their curriculum that will address • real workforce needs as opposed to graduating a plethora of students in majors where the employment opportunities are scant (journalism, philosophy, art, ethnic studies, etc.).

This education problem will get worse before it gets better. Note also we are not strictly speaking about the "U.S." either, this is a worldwide phenomena. In other words, the problem is that a pre-1990 "analog" world of limited mobile technology and no internet simply doesn't exist anymore in the digital age, and will not "come back" to as it was. Technology is here to stay. People want their social media, cell phones, online services, it is now ingrained in society.

Nonetheless, how people interface with their economies in creating personal transactions to create value is key. A UBI is not a panacea in a vacuum of value-added activity, and has real costs, that will be passed down. In other words, people have to "do something" to create value. Whether it be pushing a broom, clicks on a mouse, washing clothes, or loading a moving truck. The atomized work breakdown of activity is where value is created. Everyone is responsible for creating his/her own individualized value. A UBI cannot mask or subterfuge this socio-economic paradigm. It is as old as the stone ages, when animals were killed for food, flint used to set fires, skins traded for warmth, and tents made for shelter. Human activity to create incipient value added is part of our social DNA. Individualized actions are the currency used to create these transactions which form value. In its psychological abstract, people obtain self-worth and status from doing productive things. If this identity is removed, aberrant, antisocial behaviors can become their attribute. A UBI that infringes on its sovereign neighbors will create push/pull factors that will be hard to control economically, and with man's propensity to game systems, could lead to more illegal labor issues, with distorted economic outcomes. As we can see then, any UBI under the parameters of Westphalia will only have the effect of exclusivity, creating more push/pull factors and exacerbating the haves versus have nots problems of inequality.

NOTES

1. http://money.cnn.com/2017/05/26/news/economy/mark-zuckerberg-universal-basic-income/. Retrieved on June 2018.
2. http://basicincome.org/news/2018/12/united-states-democrats-add-basic-income-to-a-climate-change-addressing-plan/.
3. http://unctad.org/en/Pages/PressRelease.aspx?OriginalVersionID=361. Retrieved on June 2018.
4. Marx, K., et al. (1848) *The Communist Manifesto.*
5. Wright, E. O. (2005) Basic Income as a Socialist Project. *Rutgers Journal of Law & Urban Policy* 2 (Fall 1): 196–203.
6. Crozier, Michel. (2010) *The Bureaucratic Phenomenon* (with a new introduction by Erhard Friedberg). New Brunswick and London: Transactions Publishers (Originally published: Chicago: University of Chicago Press, 1964).
7. Moeller, J. O. (2016) *The Veil of Circumstance.* Singapore: ISEAS Publishing.
8. http://www.bloomberg.com/gadfly/articles/2017-01-09/the-robot-threat-donald-trump-isn-t-talking-abou?cmpid=yhoo.headline&yptr=yahoo. Retrieved on June 2018.
9. http://money.cnn.com/2017/01/30/news/economy/jobs-china-mexico-automation/?iid=EL. Retrieved on June 2018.
10. Thurow, L. (1996) *The Future of Capitalism.* New York: William Morrow & Co.; and Rifkin, J. (1995) *The End of Work.* New York: Putnam Books.
11. Polanyi, M. (1966) *The Tacit Dimension.* New York: Doubleday.
12. http://www.straitstimes.com/singapore/more-cabbies-leaving-the-job-amid-stiff-competition. Retrieved on June 2018.
13. AI, Robotics, and the Future of Jobs. Pew Research Center, August 2014. http://www.pewinternet.org/2014/08/06/future-of-jobs/.
14. Baumol, W. J. (1967) Macroeconomics of Unbalanced Growth: The Anatomy of Urban Crisis. *American Economic Review* 57 (3): 415–426.
15. Caterpillar Dodged Paying $2.4 Billion in Taxes. http://www.cnbc.com/2014/03/31/caterpillar-dodged-paying-24-billion-in-taxes-senate-report.html. Retrieved on July 2018.
16. Page, A. (2016) *Repair Versus Replace?* http://www.maintworld.com/Asset-Management/Repair-versus-Replace.

17. Autor, David H. (2015) Why Are There Still so Many Jobs? The History and Future of Workplace Automation. *Journal of Economic Perspectives* 29 (3): 3–30.
18. Universal Basic Income. http://www.cnbc.com/2017/03/25/universal-basic-income-debate-sharpens.html. Retrieved on June 2018.
19. Crozier, M. (1982) *Strategies for Change*. Cambridge, MA: MIT Press.
20. http://www.theatlantic.com/politics/archive/2015/03/welfare-makes-america-more-entrepreneurial/388598/. Retrieved on June 2018.
21. Moeller, J. (2017) *The Veil of Circumstance*, p. 208. ISEAS: Singapore.
22. http://terramagazine.terra.com.br/interna/0„OI1906421-EI6578,00. html. Retrieved on June 2018.
23. See Elon Musk, doubling down on this article, 2.13 and again. http://www.businessinsider.co.id/elon-musk-universal-basic-income-2017-2/?r=US&IR=T#sxKYLMJGA7ZIqemT.97.
24. Dambisa Moyo on Income Inequality. http://www.dw.com/en/dambisa-moyo-on-income-inequality/a-35951412.
25. http://money.cnn.com/2017/01/30/news/economy/jobs-china-mexico-automation/index.html. Retrieved on June 2018.
26. Hanlon, J., Barrientos, A., and Hulme, D. (2010) *Just Give Money to the Poor: The Development Revolution from the Global South*. Sterling, VA: Kumarian Press.
27. http://www.bbc.com/news/world-europe-36454060. Retrieved on July 2018.
28. http://www.academia.edu/31237451/THE_EFFECTIVENESS_OF_PANTAWID_PAMILYANG_PILIPINO_PROGRAM.
29. http://www.10x.co.za/faq/preservation-fund/will-all-south-africans-be-getting-a-government-pension. Retrieved on July 2018.
30. Kwon, H.-j., and Kim, W.-r. (2015) The Evolution of Cash Transfers in Indonesia: Policy Transfer and National Adaptation. *Asia and the Pacific Policy Studies* 2: 425–440. https://doi.org/10.1002/app5.83.
31. http://basicincome.org/news/2016/09/alaska-us-amount-2016-permanent-fund-dividend-1022/. Retrieved on July 2018.
32. https://www.adn.com/economy/article/first-time-years-alaskas-unemployment-rate-exceeds-nations/2014/05/17/ and http://247wallst.com/special-report/2016/11/14/the-most-dangerous-states-in-america-3/. Retrieved on June 2018.
33. http://www.fool.com/taxes/2017/11/18/whats-an-alaska-permanent-fund-dividend-and-how-ca.aspx. Retrieved on July 2018.
34. The Middle-Income Trap: Mixed-Income Myths. *The Economist*, October 17, 2017, pp. 6–8.
35. http://www.infoplease.com/world/population-statistics/world-population-milestones (UNDP statistics). Retrieved on July 2018.

36. Mayo, E. (1949) *Hawthorne and the Western Electric Company, The Social Problems of an Industrial Civilisation*. London: Routledge.
37. Bellott, F. K., and Tutor, F. D. (1990) A Challenge to the Conventional Wisdom of Herzberg and Maslow Theories. Paper presented at the Nineteenth Annual Meeting of the Mid-South Educational Research Association. New Orleans, LA.
38. Friedman, T. L. (2006) *Hot, Flat and Crowded*, p. 64. London: Penguin.
39. Dalio, R. (2015) *Economic Principles: How the Economic Machine Works*, p. 216. Bridgewater Associates.
40. http://www.livemint.com/Opinion/WrMpO95QxKF1kggt6ZrdML/The-case-against-universal-basic-income.html. Retrieved on July 2018.
41. Dalio, R., ibid., p. 1.
42. Gaming systems in organizations is written about considerably by Crozier, ibid.
43. Gray, K., and Herr, E. (1998) *Workforce Education: The Basics*. Boston: Allyn & Bacon.

CHAPTER 4

Economic Migrants and Passports

POLITICAL AND ECONOMIC MIGRANTS: ONE IN THE SAME?

Immigration is tightly linked to the backdrop of Westphalia. However, Westphalia has no profound answers to curb or abet it. The purpose of this chapter is not to debate whether immigration is based on political or economic intentions. That is for another dialogue. Nor is it to shill for open borders, a politically liberal contentious issue. Open borders are not directed at any value creation, but rather for political motives. This chapter highlights how Westphalia can cause the unintended consequences and motivations if no state borders existed. In other words, in the twenty-first century people flee from the border of one nation-state to another but big data, social media, and human rights allows them the option of never fully assimilating into their new nation-states, but rather, bringing and encapsulating their cultures and mindsets with them, via mechanisms such as language, anchor babies, chain immigration, and arranged marriages. While these things may seem minor or trivial, they do in fact lay a baseline that allows immigrants to develop parallel societies. At least for the first and possibly second generations. This is a problem that Westphalia was never equipped to deal with, but yet undermines the cohesion of its 1648 mandate, namely exclusivity.

Westphalia by its exclusivity with sovereignty creates push and pull factors with the intended and unintended consequences that are not readily understood. Consider that thousands of refugees and migrants,

W. Hickey, *The Sovereignty Game*,
https://doi.org/10.1007/978-981-15-1888-1_4

of all walks of life from laborers to medical doctors try to enter Western countries daily, by all methods: air, land, sea, tunnels, climbing fences, even bicycle.[1] Germany[2] has said it will expel several thousand Balkan economic refugees to accommodate hundreds of thousands of newly arriving asylum seekers from Syria, Afghanistan, and Iraq besieging its borders and putting significant pressure on EU countries in the Schengen agreement zone. Some EU nations are building fences and fortifying borders with fellow EU members. The EU is going out of its way to distinguish asylum seekers from economic migrants although institutional economists, which focus on how systems change behavior, have long derided attempts to handle politics and economics as exclusively discrete. In other words, the two issues cannot be separated. At the core, the issue may seem dichotomous, promoting freedom versus advancement, but appearances are deceiving.

Yet, the economy and politics are nonetheless inextricably intertwined: *All political problems are rooted in economic ones and* vice versa, argued Douglas North, who received the Nobel Prize in Economics for his theory on the "natural state" of human existence in 1990 (d. 2016). He suggested that much of the world still remains defined by personal transactions and favoritism whereby forming and enforcing agreements are limited to an exclusive group of elites. If there is no political gainsharing or democratic channels among groups in a given society, the theory suggests, those excluded rebel and seek greener pastures elsewhere, thus an economic necessity is created from a political deficiency in power-sharing arrangement. This is a problem in Westphalia, a lack of outlets for voice and opportunities of its own citizens then forces them to migrate, to other Westphalian nations, where in most cases, they will find much of the same in play.

The North theory describes Syria today, with its civil war and no economic advancement. North argued that a sustainable and open society requires enfranchisement and empowerment of all competing groups in that given society. Only a handful of countries, mostly in Scandinavia and Northern Europe, have reached this level of cognizance. Again, Westphalia is Germanic in origin. The real issues of the Balkans, for example, and transitory migrants from the Middle East, are of integration and identity. A legacy of Communism forced cultural homogeneity, and historically, the dividing line of Christian/Islamic identity has always been contentious there, (as is the identity of Muslims in predominantly Buddhist Myanmar). These are historically connotated issues that modern secularist mandates cannot neatly solve with straight lines drawn by Sykes–Picot bureaucrats in faraway places.

The issue of political refugees versus economic migrants is certainly not new, and Germany is not alone in struggling to sort out and determine who are the worthiest or neediest migrants, that is, which persons or families are deserving of asylum and who is not? This dilemma of beneficiary selection also presented itself in the last chapter about Universal Basic Income initiatives. Harvard's Michael Teitelbaum's 1980 prediction that immigrant and refugee issues would become among the most troubling issue of modern times was certainly prescient. Teitelbaum has researched international migration for the past 30 years and argues that economics (not freedom) is a strong driver among the motivations for why people migrate and become refugees. Nonetheless, that argument is lost in much of the political froth.

Teitelbaum and North each understood that economics and politics cannot be cleanly separated. There are also large gray areas, often complicated by contradictory policies, such as skilled and family-based migration. Multiple examples can be found within the context of recent mass migrations—including the Rohingya fleeing Myanmar, Syrians fleeing civil war, Sub-Saharan Africans fleeing religious violence, Tamils fleeing political retribution in Sri Lanka, Guatemalans fleeing gang and drug violence as well as North Koreans and South Sudanese fleeing brutal political oppression. Of course North and Teitelbaum both referenced everything faithfully within the borders of the nation-state, never seeming to grasp that the borders have long become blurred in the digital age.

Malcolm Turnbull, the then prime minister of Australia, proclaimed that no one arriving by boat would ever be allowed to permanently settle there. Besides Australia's controversial policy of placing illegal migrants in third countries such as Papua New Guinea, Nauru, and Cambodia for payment, he posited questions, good ones that should not be immediately dismissed as political pandering: If migration is really about refugee status, then shouldn't political obligations stop at the first safe-border of the refugee's entry? And wouldn't crossing subsequent borders implicate the political refugee as to really seeking a better life, not escaping oppression, hence rendering the political asylum process moot as an economic migrant is ultimately devolved in the process, not a refugee?

A core principle of the 1951 Refugee Convention asserts that refugees should not be returned to a country where they face serious threats to life or freedom. But as refugees cross borders in search of increasing levels of safety, the migration takes on complex legalities and a gradual process toward economic migrant status. Theoretically, a breakwater first transit by an asylum seeker in Serbia, Italy, Mexico, or Jordan could be and perhaps should be, the defining litmus of a political versus economic refugee.

Of course such a breakwater would be met with resistance by supranational (UN), ethnic, identity, and human rights groups. China, while a signatory[3] to the Convention, for example, frequently returns asylum-seeking North Koreans directly to hostile conditions as economic refugees, despite resettlement pleas by South Korea. In short, the entire issue of economic versus political refugees is very contentious.

There are several categories of countries we can consider further: embarkation and host countries depending on the reasons for migration as well as transit countries and destination countries, depending on anticipated welcome, support, and affinity either familial or diaspora.

Embarkation point	Refugee pretext	Transitory (or Breakwater)	Final destination	Affinity (diaspora)
Sri Lanka (Tamil)	Civil war/political	Indonesia/ Thailand	Australia/NZ	Low
Burma (Rohingya)	Ethnic strife	Malaysia/Thailand	Australia/NZ	Low
Syria	Civil war	Turkey/Baltics Lebanon	Germany/ Sweden	Moderate
Guatemala	Gangs/crime	Mexico	US	High
North Korea	Political oppression	China/Thailand	S. Korea	High
Sudan/Somalia	Civil war/political	Libya/Kenya	Italy/EU	N/A
Haiti	Mass poverty	Mexico/US	US/Canada	High
Afghanistan/ Iraq/Iran/Pak.	Political oppression	Turkey/Baltics/E. Europe	Germany/ Sweden	Moderate
Sub-Saharan Africa	Mass poverty/ political oppression	Spain/France	U.K.	Moderate

Source Hickey, Transit route for refugees, and path from persecution to economic refugee status with diaspora affinity in destination country

World migration numbers are on the rise, from 173 million in 2000 to 222 million in 2010 and 244 million in 2015; international law and definitions have certainly not kept pace.

Three characteristics of modern migrants are behind the rising numbers in the exodus and emigration of vast people groups:

Technologically adept—Many immigrants can manipulate technology effectively, in particular via smartphones and their applications, for cross-border activity, for example, relying on Google maps for planning their journey and social networking sites such as Facebook with its WhatsApp, to find similar members who have already made it, or to find law enforcement or rescue services who will come to their aid. Mobile phones are also used to reach out to international media, and to document their plights on camera by uploading video in real time, to showcase and highlight any abuses or mal-situations in other countries that may come their way. In short, Westphalia cannot contain information as it used to, and the migrants know it also. This also presents a conundrum of sorts for the elites and leaders in those nations. If a video goes 'viral' before they can formulate a response, public opinion can become negative or hostile.

Legally knowledgeable—Migrants are increasingly aware of Western rights and concepts including *anchor babies*, the legal right of automatic citizenship granted to any child born on US, Brazilian, or Canadian territory regardless of a parents' legal standing; chain immigration, offers of asylum in Canada, Germany, and elsewhere in the EU to those from a war-torn nations like Yemen, Afghanistan, or Syria, or the lack of a language requirement in Sweden, US, or UK to assimilate, or encapsulate, into the general population. Migrants who know their rights are empowered, and this also catches elites and officials in their nation-states off guard, whereas previously they were accustomed to dictating arbitrary rules to migrants, who had little recourse to challenge these decisions. For example, any migrant who sets foot on US soil, whether legally or illegally, has the right to file an asylum claim that must be adjudicated in a court. This can take considerable time even years, allowing the migrant to effectively set up a home in the US while awaiting a decision. Migrants are aware of this. Recently, the Trump administration in the US has tried to counter this by having asylum seekers wait in third countries until their asylum petitions can be heard in US courts, a policy that is currently enforce but under litigation from human rights groups.

Economically prudent—Migrants, even the most desperate such as Syrians fleeing their war, or Rohingya leaving Myanmar, assess the economics of staying put or going, and all cost-risk scenarios, comparing stories from friends, family, and the Internet. They decide whether to use smugglers to cross the Aegean Sea, seldom used routes through the Balkans, flights to Mexico, stopovers in Thailand or Indonesia, or bicycles to cross the Russia–Norway border in the far north. Cost always factors into these decisions on whether to use smugglers or strike out on their own, should they take a bus or a €500 taxi, try a rubber dinghy, or pay more for a speedboat, or even fly first class, where border controls are less stringent, and even welcoming, for the well-heeled.

We can see from the above three situations, refugees are using information and data to circumvent traditional Westphalian means of people control. This is important: they have mastered the data available to them in real time. The world grows smarter, and more aware of what they can and need to do.

Still, sympathy can decline over time. There are delays in registration and rough treatment along with minimal education, health care, or employment provisions, even though the Refugee Convention outlines basic standards for treatment including access to courts, primary education, work, and travel documents similar to passports. The Convention is just that, a treaty, only as strong as the weakest Westphalian adherent. Some Western countries such as Germany hold the convention in high regards, others such as Poland and Hungary, not so much.

Countries have discovered that their generosity attracts an overwhelming number of refugees and seeks to discourage migrants by making deals with developing nations (i.e., outsourcing their people problems) and insisting that refugees cannot pursue multiple border crossings and still be considered a refugee. Thus, a German bound Syrian refugee under threat of war in his home country could forfeit this claim to political refugee status after setting foot in Turkey or Jordan. Nonetheless, human rights groups have cried foul at trying to enforce this dialectic too aggressively.

As Syrians, Afghans, and Iranians pass through the EU's Greece, Hungary, and Bulgaria on their way to Germany, their claims to persecution do in fact quickly diminish, however unpalatable that may seem to many activists. Whether it be Rohingyas in Bangladesh or Syrians stranded in Serbia, or Sri Lankans in Indonesia, the United Nations and governments are trying an impossible task of establishing definitions for economic versus political refugees. The lines have become blurred, with the ultimate decisions, predisposed to cultural and historical prejudices. We can see that North's natural state argument then about political and economic issues being mirror images is genuine.

PAY FOR PASSPORTS

We now turn our discussion to an area that denominates Westphalia into real outcomes in peoples lives, though theoretically in the era of big data and social media, it shouldn't: Passports. What are passports exactly? They are travel documents that give the holder the permission from his or her

Westphalian state to enter into another Westphalian state by reciprocity of acceptance and safe passage. Meaning country A accepts passport holders with a visa from country B, and vice versa. The passport still defines the person, not their skills or their abilities. While this should not be, it is an overwhelming "is". People are denominated, and paid, by where they are from. Not always for what they can do.

The writer has found in living abroad that salaries and by extension privilege and respect levels are all ultimately denominated in the passport. This is the true Westphalian exclusivity ideal, but not the current world trend. German, Singaporean, Japanese passport holders are considered the best and brightest the world has to offer even if they have no skills. Yemeni, Sri Lankan, Congolese, are considered the flotsam and jetsam of the developing world, even if they can code for the blockchain. Even the US is not considered the world's best passport holder. They have fallen many levels due to making enemies abroad. Swiss, Swedes, and Norwegians have no enemies. They are welcome everywhere. Afghanis and Cambodians not so much. Chinese, due to their spending power, have passports that are on the rise. Conversely, Argentines and Venezuelans, once rich, but now considered the beggars of South America.

The point of all this is not to discuss which passports have more or less power, or to praise or insult the holder, but that the individual, no matter how talented, or conversely how ignorant, is ultimately anchored to that document. A dumb German engineer is considered as superior to a highly trained Filipino one, even though the Filipino engineer may have years of experience and expertise, and the German engineer a novice, his salary is ultimately defined by that passport. Further, international companies actually index their pay policies to so-called "local labor conditions", this is a euphemism to discriminate on salaries based on passports. Meaning that 20 year plus experienced Filipino engineer on a Manila index of local salaries would be considered well-compensated at say, $1200 a month, whereas a newly recruited, fresh out of university, German engineer, on a Frankfurt index, would be considered low paid at only euro 5000 ($6000) per month. The companies justify this economic racism as their current acceptable domestic rating, i.e., paying for their passport. Even if the Filipino engineer is the superior to the German one, the salary range will still stand. The passport is still the main mechanism of control for the Westphalian nation-state.

But people are not fooled, they can now easily search online or via social media what the true pay trends are how much the skills themselves, not the passports or citizenship, should be compensated for. Of course companies do not like to discuss this, and demur when asked what their compensation policies are, but the facts speak for themselves, namely, they can no longer hide behind Westphalian constructs in a world of social media and big data. Information flows freely, people demand equal pay for similar skills. To take this a step further, if one visits Dubai, Bangkok, Hong Kong, or Singapore, one notes the vast amounts of foreign labor imported from impoverished areas of Myanmar, Nepal, and the Philipines. Local residents in those places shun hard labor. It must be imported. We consider then that artificial walls are created to insulate and uphold one group, while marginalizing and trivializing the other. The passport defines the holder. Not the motivations, skills, or abilities of the other. Essentially, the nation-state then becomes the purveyor of institutionalized racism and bias. Telling people they can 'eventually become a citizen of another nation' is not the definitive, here and now, answer many seek with equality and for human rights.

The discussion of this is not to denigrate individuals or people groups, but rather to highlight how Westphalia still siloes and sidelines particular groups. Nonetheless, it is still how people are warehoused, rewarded, or rejected. The passport is the prima facie indicator of Westphalia. That will not change anytime soon, though in a digital age that rewards human capital, its relevance is under scrutiny.

In the twenty-first century we need a new system that cannot be gamed for either immigration or salaries. This may sound overly simplistic, but Westphalia cannot address immigration in a natural form, namely it forms human barriers that are no longer relevant in today's digital world. Enormous amounts of money, resources, policing, and effort are still spent to maintain and enforce artificial borders that people use their intelligence of the laws, social situation, and landscape to get around. Further, some smart people are handicapped by their nation-state, whereas others are rewarded for simply being in theirs. This does not fit neatly into an empowered digital economy based on knowledge.

NOTES

1. People leaving Russia to enter Norway in the Arctic Circle are not permitted to enter on foot. Without a car, a bicycle will suffice.
2. http://www.infomigrants.net/en/post/3474/types-of-protection-in-germany-for-asylum-seekers. Retrieved on November 2017.
3. http://www.unhcr.org/uk/3b73b0d63.pdf. Retrieved on November 2017.

CHAPTER 5

Reforming State-Owned Enterprises

*State-Owned Companies are an arm of the state, are not
profit-driven entities, and distort the normal business playing field*

Under the Westphalian system, certain organizations in predominantly
socialist and communist countries, called State-Owned Enterprises
(SOEs), thrive and employ thousands of people.[1] The main problem
with SOEs is that under this rubric they can and do distort free market economics, on which so many of the worlds Democracies depend.
Much of the world's SOE involvement has been driven by an economically ascendant China, but large state-owned companies also exist and
distort economies in Brazil, Russia, Indonesia, India, and South Africa,
to name a few.

SOEs are a tangible extension of the Westphalian nation-state, and fall
under state capitalism not market-driven economics. State capitalism can
alter the concept of the nation-state as it allows government and business
to become one, whereby other countries simply cannot compete against
a combined state and commercial actor. At the core of state capitalism,
SOEs provide the traditional "social contract" for citizens in a nation-
state that is usually bereft in many privatized for-profit companies seeking
lower wages and creating competitive products. There has been a steady
drumbeat from many multilateral institutions about developing countries
needing to dismantle their SOEs, and so much has been written about this

topic[2] to thoroughly muddy the waters, but SOE reform is quite politically complicated. It becomes a purview of the exclusivity of the Westphalian nation-state. Namely, nation-states running companies to control lucrative domestic businesses, such as oil, electricity, banking, telecommunications, insurance, infrastructure, and even hotels. While SOEs in many countries are only interested in their own domestic markets, a recent trend has been in their outward bound investments. China in particular with its "One-belt, One-road" (now called "Belt and Road") initiative is all about expanding its footprint internationally to gain more work and projects for its vast SOE network which is facing growth and employment constraints at home. But other countries SOEs are also going abroad such as Saudi Aramco in Saudi Arabia, Petronas in Malaysia, and Rosneft in Russia. It is noted these are all energy companies, largely in search of more commodity resources but also in expanding national influence abroad.

Structural Reforms

There are SOEs all over the developing world, but China is considered as the world's heavyweight poster boy of SOEs due to its enormous economy and its raft of SOEs that are subsidized and protected by the government to insulate massive amounts of unskilled and redundant workers from being laid off or fired.[3] Nonetheless, many countries have behemoth SOEs, mostly in fossil fuels, that also employ millions of redundant and unnecessary workers simply to keep political stability, isolated from international competitive factors. For example, the Indian National Railway is India's largest employer, Saudi Aramco is a cradle to grave employer in Saudi Arabia, Petrobras in Brazil is that nation's largest employer. This domestic monopoly situation only serves to hinder, not promote, the necessary economic competitiveness and innovation needed to develop their economies further. Despite all the talk about necessary reform of SOEs, they are still there, entrenched as ever in their business models, even if the industry is a loss maker, nation-state governments order their banks to continue loaning to them.

The main problem with SOEs is that they distort the way traditional business is done. Since the actors are not for profit, profits do not matter, or should we say, are not the ultimate endgame. They can dump product, engage in unfair labor practices, and expand their markets artificially as they have no bottom line, except employment. In certain industries, such as steelmaking, textiles, and resources, for-profit companies simply cannot compete against a state sponsored behemoth. SOEs only accountability is to their respective Westphalian governments not customers, and to create the political and economic stability and certainty the leaders and their elites crave. It is acknowledged many governments have gone on long press campaigns to make their SOEs profitable, efficient, and market oriented, but so much of this is just that, a press release. At the end of the day, change is slow if nonexistent, and reversion to the mean the usual outcome.

Any rapid retrenchment or reform of SOEs will result in chaos and instability. Essentially, the reforms being proposed may be too strong medicine for some troubled economies. Perhaps a way forward regarding SOEs is in acknowledging them as domestic employment generators, instead of in Western "competitiveness" conceptual frameworks. Nonetheless, without acknowledgment of this Westphalian state industry problem, there can be no meaningful reform. State-owned companies manifest a tangible mantra of Westphalia in a way it was never intended, namely a well-protected monopoly that can bulldoze its way over other smaller or poorer Westphalian states economies.[4]

One-party and socialist governance systems simply do not have the political "go along to get along" required in democracies for approval of all aspects of doing business. What many Western business leaders may not clearly grasp is that profit and loss statements and revenue streams are secondary, perhaps tertiary, to unelected or authoritarian leaders who at the controls can create wealth through various artifices that the state will control and compensate, not the public.

This is state capitalism. It is direct. It is efficient. It is powerful. It is not beautiful, and certainly not inclusive. It provides those elites in control with many levers across many levels of power: municipal, provincial, and national. Power concedes nothing without demand. Demands come from social awareness, a critical press, and deeper understanding of the issues. That is something that many of these nation-states can ill afford to gamble on, nevermind tolerate.

The argument herein presented is twofold, first, political considerations, namely social capital building which is predicated on trust, and second, technical ability. In both cases, it will reinforce why these countries, and China in particular, cannot wean itself from its monopoly reliance on SOEs and also on the "fixed investment" export model (mostly to Western consumers), that has been a highly successful growth driver for the past 30 years but is now hurting many countries long-term economic prospects in their failure to develop a consumption-led domestic services industry.

Many economists and business leaders feel these nation-states will be responsible players under a service-oriented market economy. How they err: this is wishful thinking. They fail to acknowledge one glowering internal contradiction, namely, service economies require discussion, transparency, critical thinking, and public discourse to exchange ideas and compare and critique, all things which they, and in particular, China's one-party state frowns upon. To this end, it also answers why people in these countries save so much money, and how a debt-fueled services economy cannot fully emerge: people simply don't trust their government's promises about the future.

However, we consider the raw infrastructure ability of SOEs in one-party states, and projects. China now offers it all and is opening itself up to the developing world. Just to name a few things for relevance, and how these things could upgrade any developing countries "progress curve" overnight, some issues which even the US and other Western countries have not excelled at yet, due to regulations and political deadlock found in their own nation-state exclusivity.

Floating nuclear power plants. This is at the conjecture stage, but no doubt doable. This idea has been promoted to create power for China's politically contentious island development plan in the South China Sea. China is already exporting nuclear power plants to the developing worlds. Cheaper, and more efficiently than Western companies. Of course safety is another issue.

Maglev Trains and high-speed railway. High-speed rail now dots the Chinese country. Even third level cities are getting the "CRH" G train, which can hit speeds over 300 kph. A recent proposal for example, by entreprenuer Elan Musk to develop a high-speed rail corridor connecting Los Angeles with San Francisco for example has been shelved due to spiraling costs, environmental and land rights concerns. Which country would be better suited in an age of high-cost labor and regulatory approval to model and build this in a developing country would be a good example.

Gigantic hydroelectric dams that can generate gigawatts, not megawatts of reliable baseload power. Think about the Three Gorges on the Yangtze river and the Mekong river dam projects. Both have been very contentious, especially to downstream countries, but in a one-party state it is not open to discussion.

The Hong Kong–Macau–Zhuhai bridge. This project, now completed, showcases man-made islands and a tunnel between the special China administrative regions of Macau and Hong Kong. If one lands at the Hong Kong International airport, the immensity of this project is on full display with pylons, and concrete foundations as far as one can see. Since many developing countries such as Indonesia, Sri Lanka, and Nicaragua have large expanses of water to cover, building them has its own instilled demand. It would seem then that exporting products are not the ultimate concern, but rather projects. Unfortunately, due to cross-border issues with China, Macau, and Hong Kong this project has not reached full capacity, and is doubtful it will anytime soon, it runs the risk of becoming a white elephant.

All countries want to develop quickly and China has both the financial largesse with its trillions of dollars held in reserve and ability to do it, in part to their savings rate, and in their construction ability with their creation of their various international banks (BoC, ICBC, CBoC) as a type of multinational Development Bank, without the strings attached by the usual actors: Wall St. with dollar-denominated bond issues, the World Bank with social and environmental requirements, NGO and "aid" organizations that may have some political mandate behind them. Faustian bargains for the investee countries? To be certain, but doable nonetheless. Financing now of the export model to "take it abroad" is the conveyance, while badly needed infrastructure (bridges, toll roads, airports, power plants, etc.) in the developing world is the reward.

Market Versus Controlled Economies

The main point then, is why would China's or other leaders want to gamble on a capitalist system of providing value-added services when they can have it all, by enlarging the capital investment model in other countries, and by taking a page from the IMF/World Bank playbook: financing the projects themselves, to give the business to their own SOEs? Service economies, on the other hand and by their nature are at the beck and call of a fickle public, international competition, and the attendant inspection that the public puts into these organizations.

This is not to say a service economy is not important, quite the contrary, if societies want to advance to higher levels of responsibility with value-added products and services (think UK Lloyds insurance, Australian education, Swiss watches, and even the US McDonalds/Coke pairing), these are all trusted brands where consumers expect a certain standard of results. But that is under a capitalist economy, not a state-controlled one. China in fact does welcome a market economy.... except for certain so-called "strategic industry" which can carry a very broad definition, and that is where the SOE capital investment model reigns supreme: telecom, energy, banking, and airlines. If one grows rice, printing T-shirts, opening a coffee shop, or making boutique handbags, a market economy in many of these countries is very welcome, but if producing oil, building bridges or sharing nuclear technology, a market economy will take a back seat to the needs of the exclusivity of the nation-state, and the powerful elites vested with the control of those interests.

But semantics aside, many of these leaders have a more pressing problem on their hands: Mass unemployment that could lead to social unrest and directly affecting their political tenure, is the main driver in supporting ongoing SOE enterprise. A problem confronting all developing Westphalian nations. Developing a service-oriented economy predicated on trust, social awareness, and the legal certainties the public demands takes time. The service economy meanwhile can be outsourced to foreigners, and that is exactly what is happening.

Many of these countries are going to continue to export...it's all they know, just not goods such as steel and plastic gadgets, but now projects under a "Blue Oceans" capital investment strategy to a hungry developing world that is in now tune with the Internet and social media, new cars, bigger houses, consumer brands, and better lifestyles that all desperately need power and infrastructure to attain....and quickly. China and other countries SOEs won't be building dams, roads, nuclear power plants, and Maglev trains domestically alone, but also for foreign parties, in particular, for Africa, which has need for the most upgrades and can offer large amounts of raw commodities in return.

Will these have repercussions and spillovers for the planet? Most certainly. If unchecked, China is pursuing an irresponsible path in world events that is allowable under (or openly challenging?) the seventeenth-century Westphalian construct of nation-state governance as a "sovereignty" right of non-interference in its internal affairs, a theme that is echoed in China *ad nausea*. At the time of Westphalia in 1648, there was certainly no concept of state capitalism or the behemoth nature of the entirety of the state, both legally and economically, unless one considers the British East India Company, there are really no other comparisons. That would begin with the Communist revolution of 1918 and creation of the USSR. Nonetheless this path of SOE has a high cost for the planet, in terms of the looming issues of climate change, resource depletion, and safety issues (i.e., nuclear power plant safety, and now China's extra-territorial maritime claims in still largely acknowledged international waters).

This is not to mention China's political leaders have instilled in their people the Schadenfreude implications of attaining >6% yearly gross domestic product economic growth "at all costs". Changing China (and other countries) to a truly market-driven economy and transitioning from the export model is crucial, but right now, that is not a prerogative of the Beijing leadership which has other economic tools on hand to protect its power, such as currency devaluation. To increase the export model, outwardly, simply requires a small change in government strategy, but to change to a domestic services economy requires a sea change in the public mindset.

PUBLIC–PRIVATE PARTNERSHIPS (PPP'S)

PPPs or Public-Private Partnerships, are the blurring of the lines between private (for-profit) business and state-controlled business, in particular for energy and infrastructure projects. Much fanfare has been given to PPPs from India to Russia to Indonesia, nonetheless, the results have been minimal at best. Simply, most private companies do not want a public partner that they will have to train, manage, and pay for if things go wrong, especially when (not if) governments move the goalposts of definitions of project success or unilaterally change contract terms, which they do. Guarantees from the state side are in order, in particular for any megaprojects. Only state-owned enterprises, with the backing of the state are in any position to take on such vast projects as infrastructure investment is costly. A recent report by McKinsey estimated that US$57 trillion in infrastructure investment is required between now and 2030 to simply keep pace with global GDP growth.[5] For economic infrastructure alone, that report said, Asia will require almost US$8 trillion (Fig. 5.1).

Attracting private investors requires bankable projects: developments that will reliably deliver private sector investors their principle and promised returns. (McKinsey 2018)

There are also many other large numbers. No governments can meet these capital needs, not even China by itself. In fact, Chinas' largess as of this writing may actually be slowing, and a repudiation of projects, such as the East Coast railway in Malaysia, the Kuala Lumpur-Singapore High Speed line, or the Colombo port in Sri Lanka has occured when domestic

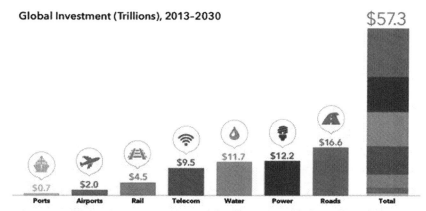

Fig. 5.1 Global investment in infrastructure needs through 2030 (*Source* McKinsey)

political actors lost power.[6] Clearly, the private sector must play a role, but attracting private investors requires very bankable projects: developments that will reliably deliver returns to private sector investors their capital. To be clear, investing in any PPPs means investing alongside the government via their SOEs, there is no way around it.

This also means all governments will have to behave, prioritizing the selection of infrastructure opportunities and ensuring good governance. That is the ideal. Additionally, to live within tight capital constraints, governments have to learn to be economical in implementation, raising productivity and driving innovations in developing country infrastructure. This is where smaller IPPs (Independent Power Producers) can make inroads. Of course, in any such huge state-controlled projects, corruption is a constant issue, in particular in nation-states in Africa where governance and institutions are weak and corruption sits high on the index.

China's SOEs Create a New Paradigm

As stated, China's SOEs represent the largest tangible investment vehicles, or "engines", that are now going abroad to actually do the work, many being financed by the AIIB or "Asian Infrastructure Investment Bank", 亚投行 (the Chinese equivalent to the IMF or World Bank). In essence, China is going to use its $3 trillion plus in foreign reserves to fund its own international expansion, using its preferred domestic investment and mass jobs creator of the SOE, going abroad.[7] This is something that other, market-based economies are simply unable to deal with or realize the ramifications of. Consider that many companies are hamstrung by their own nation-state governments over environmental, political, or human rights concerns that do not preclude Chinese SOEs from investing in places such as in African or South American dictatorships, or central Asian economies where corruption is rife. In all these places, environmental protections are rarely, if ever, prioritized.

Therefore, much of the heavy construction, financing, and project upbraiding will be done by Chinese SOEs (Table 5.1), which are in turn backstopped by Beijing and its massive foreign exchange war chest. SOEs, as a rule, are usually vertically contained organizations (from laborers to mechanical engineers) operating megaprojects of everything from dams,[8] to refineries, high-speed rail, upstream oil production, mine development, ports, and bridges. Yet, public relations, communications, marketing, and media outlets (i.e., the communications services necessary for acceptance) for Chinese SOEs, remain in their infancy. Smaller and nimbler private companies, by way of entrepreneurism, need to be able to take the initiative to identify key SOE decision-makers, and introduce themselves and their services to these behemoth entities, as they will not actively recruit or solicit outsiders without direct central government orders from Beijing, or significant previous relationship bonds usually formed via joint ventures in China with trusted Western partners, like Siemens, GE or ABB.

While many opportunities still do exist for companies worldwide, knowing how to involve them in and what countries to entertain them in, is still very fluid. SMEs in particular, are more suitable for these type of "on the fly" projects than large capitalized Western energy firms such as an Exxon, Mitsubishi, Samsung, Shell, or BHP Billiton, that require longer timelines and defined IRRs, (internal rates of return) and may also be politically compromised, as SOEs are politically controlled contrivances, and are not driven by the quarterly statement (as many Western publicly traded energy and infrastructure consortia projects are). However, SOEs are still under political deadlines to complete projects, and there exist considerable opportunities for savvy and flexible SMEs (small and medium-sized enterprises) therefore to work with these SOEs that can demonstrate proficiency in two core areas, standards and localization.

Table 5.1 Profile sampling of SOE employment for Chinese infrastructure/energy companies

China SOE	Approx. # employees	Type of business
State Grid 国家电网公司	1,600,000	Electricity T&D
Huaneng Power 华能集团公司	103,000	Electricity utility
Shanghai Electric 海电气	28,000	Electricity T&D
China Southern Power 南方电网	130,000	Electricity T&D
Guodian Power 国电集团公司	110,000	Electricity utility
China Resources 华润 公司	40,000	Coal
Datong Coal 大同煤矿集团公司	200,000	Coal
China Shenhua 神华能源公司	75,000	Coal
Anhui Cement 安徽海螺水泥股份	40,000	Cement
HBIS 河北钢铁集团有限公司	124,000	Steel
Shougang Steel 首钢	75,000	Steel making equipment
Bao Steel 宝钢集团公司	108,000	Steel
Sinopec 石油化工集团公司	359,000	Downstream oil and gas
CNPC PetroChina 石油 公司	1,600,000	Upstream oil and gas
CNOOC 海洋石油总公司	100,000	Offshore oil and gas
Sinochem 中化集团公司	50,000	Chemicals/refineries
CRCC 铁道建筑总公司	254,000	Rail
COSCO 远洋运输	130,000	Shipping and ports
Sinohydro 水电	135,000	Port and dams
CMC 机械进出口	38,000	Power plants and roads
	Sample Avg: ~265,000	
	Sample Total: ~5.3 million	
	Range: 28,000–1.6 million	
By comparison		
Walmart (Worldwide)	2.1 million	
McDonalds (including Franchisees)	1.7 million	
Indian National Railway (SOE)	1.4 million	
General Electric	303,000	

Source Hickey
World Economic Forum, Chinese SOE Websites

STANDARDS

Chinese SOE standards are not always congruent with internationally accepted standards, such as ASME for products, API in oil, SGR in railways, or TAFE in mining. Beijing, as financier for its SOEs, at times wants to exclusively use its own standards, such as its GB (guobiao, 国标), standard for products, versus any internationally accepted ISO, whereby the two standards may not overlap. Understanding parts and equipment adaptation, such as different cycles (60 Hz v. 50 Hz) in Western versus Asian power plants, to various challenging environmental conditions (such as volcanic areas, swamps, deserts, and jungles) and possible shortcuts toward least resistance from equipment tolerance for electric transmission or LNG hookups, to safety (NEBOSH), vocational such as NSQ,[9] or to local content requirements to various civil codes in specific countries, can give energy vendors a valuable "*niche knowledge*" in working with SOEs. Further, the advent and use of 5G will set new telecommunications standards, which is really a race right now between China and the US. China simply cannot operate in vacuum, and host governments will ultimately demand international integration beyond Chinese standards alone. This is a paramount concept, foreign countries want internationally recognized "ways of doing things", i.e. Soviet and obscure standards are out of date, and serve the individual nation-state, not efficiency. In short, standards need to converge worldwide to deal with pressing issues, not diverge.

LOCALIZATION

This area is comprised of three highly interconnected areas for political acceptance and gainsharing in all host countries

Technology Transfer—The days of "black boxes" or specialty techniques that no others have access to, are sunsetting due to the Internet, patent expirations, and widespread, instantaneous communications. To make projects politically palatable in countries with large (and usually unskilled) populations, relevant, appropriate, and current technology transfer is mandated via an action plan. Many cutting edge SMEs as their niche advantage, carry these best practices that many leviathan sized SOEs with slow, highly bureaucratic organizations simply can't do.

Local Content Delivery—Similar to tech transfer initiatives, large imports of foreign-made specialty goods such as piping for refineries, robots for tank cleaning, turbines for power plants, compressor trains, pipeline pigs, or specialty bits for oil drilling, and conveyors for mining are no longer blindly accepted with host countries governments footing the bill for these products at full retail prices. Many countries now have local content requirements, including labor components, and domestic or even on-site fabrication, from turbines, to boilers, to steel production, for example, and these areas are closely monitored for infractions. SMEs with a demonstrated local content knowledge of parts or equipment could contract with SOEs to meet this requirement. To further this, and as an advantage, SMEs with carbon mitigation plans or renewable initiatives would be in better situated to demonstrate holistic local content development with any investing SOEs. In other words, host countries can demand clean and up to date technology. To that end, any SOE that does not have a clean energy or "green" profile would be suspected and implicated of using older, inefficient technologies. Host countries need to be on their guard about being sold obsolete or heavily polluting technology, or surplus inventory the SOE cannot unload to its domestic customers.

Skills Development—As with local content, influxes of armies of skilled foreign workers in resource-rich countries but with high unemployment rates and weak educational systems (such as in Angola, Yemen, or Sudan) are especially loathed and a major cause of political friction with projects. A demonstrated localization plan, which trains and puts locals in defined supervisory and management positions on projects over a timeline, will greenlight projects more quickly than any financial largess or politically empty talk about "PPPs" alone. China also knows this, but with a insular engineering culture, and limited public relations experience, are have trouble articulating a clear vision.

So how does all this sum up regarding Westphalia? Simply, we have a new paradigm, where state capitalism becomes a worldwide driver of economic growth bereft of controls from other Western nation-states with market-oriented economies that are not monopolistic or predatory. To solve the issues of the public goods dilemma, a problem that everyone owns, but no one takes ownership of, is that there must be convergences of practices, standards, and legal certainty, not divergence. But divergence is precisely what is happening. State-owned companies, not well understood in developed countries, are a creation of the Westphalian nation-state. They operate on a different level than that of for-profit, market-driven companies that must compete collectively with limited government support. Working independently, with the state as guarantor, they are beholden to no other entities on the rationale of exclusivity. SOEs are simply not profit-driven, despite any proclamations to the contrary. SOEs need reform in areas of social responsibility (CSR), standards, and in particular addressing corruption, both in their systems and in the countries they do business with. SMEs are considered as a possible first step to engagement with SOEs to triangulate standards and localization initiatives. In other words, to prevent SOEs from becoming strictly government to government (G2G) transactions, they must engage smaller market-driven players with a strong local knowledge and competency to get to success. That again is the ideal, the reality hides within Westphalia, which is now used conveniently as a distortion entity.

Notes

1. Economist Special Edition, January 2012, *State Capitalism.*
2. http://press-files.anu.edu.au/downloads/press/p212991/pdf/ch056.pdf. Retrieved on March 2019.
3. http://fortune.com/2015/07/22/china-global-500-government-owned/. Retrieved on March 2019.
4. Of course one may accuse the British in the eighteenth century and later the US in the nineteenth century, of setting the tone, but in both those cases, business entities, be it the British East India Company or Standard Oil had to eventually demonstrate profits to investors, but not SOEs!
5. http://www.capitalgroup.com/asia/insights-landing/investment_insights/articles/infrastructure-bill-due.html.
6. http://finance.yahoo.com/news/china-apos-pockets-may-not-182700308.html. Retrieved on April 2019.
7. Hanlon, Robert J. (2017) Thinking About the Asian Infrastructure Investment Bank: Can a China-Led Development Bank Improve Sustainability in Asia? *Asia and the Pacific Policy Studies* 4 (3): 541–554.
8. Yeophantong, P. (2014) China's Lancang Dam Cascade and Transnational Activism in the Mekong Region: Who's Got the Power? *Asian Survey* 54 (4): 700–724.
9. http://www.nebosh.org.uk   and   http://www.msde.gov.in/nsqf.html. Retrieved on April 2019.

CHAPTER 6

Westphalia and Finance: The "Cramdown" of Devaluation and Sovereign Bonds

You have meddled with the primal forces of nature Mr. Beale, and I won't have it! Is that clear? You think you have merely stopped a business deal, that is not the case… it is ebb and flow, tidal gravity, it is ecological balance. You are an old man who thinks in terms of 'nations' and 'peoples', there are no nations, there are no peoples…there is only one holistic system of systems… the multinational dominion of dollars… It is the international system of currency that determines the totality of life on this planet… that is the natural order of things TODAY! And YOU WILL ATONE! There is no America, there is no Democracy. We no longer live in a world of nations and ideologies. Life is a business, Mr. Beale, and it has been that way ever since man crawled out of the slime…[1]

The Westphalian nation-state is a seventeenth-century construct that is technically obsolete in today's modern age but is still held as sacred by all nation-state participants involved. All currency derives its value from the sovereign system, or nation-state, in which it exists, or in a shared system of sovereignty such as the European Union. The individual is held hostage to their decisions. Central banks, or the national bank of any given sovereign or region-sovereign area like the European Unions Central Bank, in Frankfurt, control the money supply and interests rates. Nonetheless, shared systems can also generate severe internal economic disruptions such as Greece and Italy using the euro, thee slower or deficit economies cannot keep up with more productive ones, such as Germany or the Benelux which are industrial exporting powerhouses.

© The Author(s) 2020
W. Hickey, *The Sovereignty Game*,
https://doi.org/10.1007/978-981-15-1888-1_6

This chapter is not about rehashing unwinnable arguments between the Keynesian school (liberal economic policy) or the Austrian school (conservative fiscal policy). Rather this chapter is a 3rd point focus on what really underpins the value of currency in the twenty-first century: that is, perceptions of value. Is it a perception defined by political fiat, commodity reserves (like oil), holding another country's currency such as in dollars or Swiss francs in vast foreign exchange reserves, military prowess, such as nuclear weapons, or technological know-how such as high-end gadgets (a smartphone like Apple or electric cars, like Tesla) all in the context of the Westphalian nation-state? In other words, what makes the inherent value of a nation-state's currency acceptable as a store of value worldwide, conversely, what are the factors that make another nation-state's currency less valuable (inequality, poverty, overprinting, high current account deficits, etc.). Much of this is also linked to the preeminence of the dollar, which stands hidden behind the Oz curtain as the ultimate store of value to which all other systems bow to.

ODE TO MURRAY ROTHBARD: THE NIELSEN RATINGS

The late institutional economist Murray Rothbard has had his critics in that he considered currencies and gold in particular in a very simplistic monetary environ, bereft of the high velocity of monetary transactions in the world around us and the infinitesimal amount of financial liabilities worldwide. In other words, Rothbard was for dumbing down the entire system, which had grown far too complex, even in the 1960s, when he wrote his seminal "What is Money". Nonetheless, Rothbard did force a rethink of the entire concept of "*what is money*". No paper money has value in and of itself except for what people subscribe to believing it has. It is an ethereal identity that is assigned an ascribed value by world markets. Similarly, the Nielsen ratings of television shows worldwide are based on a set sampling of subscriber boxes in spatially sectored homes. The "value" of the show then is taken by how many people in the sample size tune into it. That is then extrapolated to the public at large. The keynote in Rothbard's seminal work is that public policy simply cannot be set without understanding money and the government's ability to undermine its value in order to cover its ever-growing expanding costs, albeit with more paper currency. This is done in order to avoid structural reforms that would ultimately increase competitiveness.

The dollar is the world's effective "international currency" that replaced the gold standard Murray Rothbard spoke of in his book.[2] Rothbard's view of the world was very US-centric, as were most economic works at the time, as the 1950s onward, was the zenith of US economic power and industrial prestige following WWII.

The Devaluation Game: Currency Is as Much Qualitative as Quantitative

Currency is the tangible nameplate of the nation-state. It represents its store of value on paper. A currency devaluation is when the money is cheapened to appease domestic (exclusive) obligations on its own people, or anyone holding that particular currency. Devaluation is a rich mans game using the levers of the Westphalian state to effectively force a "cramdown" for its largess and fiscal mismanagement (i.e., vote-buying, entitlement, and welfare programs, unreformed labor markets, excessive and unneccesary military hardware purchases) on uneducated and marginalized populations. However, devaluations fool no one in the modern age of instantaneous information anymore.[3] This issue is still lost on most orthodox economists who consider devaluation as a way to balance the books via this "cramdown" on the lowest common denominator of a country: its citizens.

Gresham's Law states that bad money drives out good money, and vice versa. In currency valuation, Gresham's Law states that if a new coin ("bad money") is assigned the same face value as an older coin containing a higher amount of precious metal ("good money"), then the new coin will be used in circulation while the old money will eventually disappear from circulation and be hoarded. In part, this is why people buy dollars, and hoard them, they have little trust in their Westphalian fiat currencies, or "bad money" that is foisted on them. The reality is however, the dollar is also an imperfect fiat currency.

Collapse of the Austrian Empire and Weimar Germany

A short overview of the Austrian Empire's collapse after WWI and the subsequent war reparations Germany had to pay after the war is in order. Both events had world impacts on currency issues that still exist today, namely issues of *"currency controls"*[4] and *"currency overprinting"*. Differentials in currency values and quantities of that currency (a wheelbarrow of German marks to buy a loaf of bread for example)[5] create incentives for people to move money in or out of countries or regions (i.e., Hong Kong and China, where rich Chinese on the mainland seek to get their money out to maintain its value before it is manipulated by its China Central Bank (PBOC), whereas Hong Kong, with its imported US monetary policy, then becomes a more stable foundation to place their wealth). When the Ottoman Empire collapsed in 1916, it had different areas with different currency values. People wanted to dump their weaker currencies in favor of stronger ones. The government resorted to canceling notes, searching people at borders, and stamping old notes with newer (and lesser) values. This is Gresham's law in effect[6] which we previously mentioned. After WWI, in Weimar Germany, the government began to print money in excess to cover war reparations owed to the allies (there is some disagreement academically about the real reasons). The effect was the Weimar Republic mark became worthless in a hyperinflative environment. Also noted is the ongoing carnage caused by overprinting of money (hyperinflation) in countries from Zimbabwe with its 100 trillion note,[7] to Nigeria, to Argentina, to Egypt, to Venezuela bolivars where 3000 bolivars is now worth about 6 US cents on the black market. These issues under the Westphalian nation-state construct, have never been clearly resolved or disappeared. Today, we see the effects of currency controls (effectively the control of banknotes after a political change or mandate) everywhere from China to India to even the US, with its limits on capital outflows limited to $10,000 unless declared to the US Treasury. Nation-states simply do not want their money, or wealth, leaving in times of political uncertainty, or hot money flooding in for unregulated opportunity during economic booms. However, people are not fooled like a few decades ago, they can quickly communicate via social media cross-border to determine the real state of affairs. They discuss ways to get their money out and circumvent Westphalia.

Plaza Accord 1985

We recognize that while the 1980s were a time of information explosion, they were still pre-internet. People on the street did not clearly know what was happening with their money like in today's digitally apprised world. Perhaps the last great foolscap of the Westphalian world was the Plaza Accord held at the Plaza hotel in New York in 1985. In this situation, worldwide over ascription to the US dollar, in a time of great economic uncertainty, led to it becoming so overvalued that the US Treasury went to other industrialized countries pleading with them to weaken it. This was caused when US central banker Paul Volker had raised interest rates so high to combat inflation that the US dollar became a magnet for international investment opportunity. Conversely, the overvalued dollar began to cripple US industry. The result of the Plaza Accord's dollar devaluation was a windfall for the Japanese yen and German mark. The yen alone appreciated over 50% between 1985 and 1987 due to this political meddling. But the case point of this chapter shows that the exclusivity of the Westphalian system **could indeed** be overridden if market forces underpinned by a store of wealth (dollars) and their elites demanded it.[8] What is ironic with the Plaza Accord is that most Westphalian states suffer from devaluing currencies in relation to the dollar due to statist political structural forces that they cannot change. In this case, the Plaza Accord begged them to strengthen their money to correspondingly making the dollar weaker.

THE HANKE CONUNDRUM: CAN THE BLIND LEAD THE BLIND?

We note from the above discussions that all is abstracted in ultimate US dollar values. It is taken as a normal, in fact, an accepted, without question, denominator. Every currency or financial report is always measured in "per dollar" terms. The US dollar is above reproach. Stephen Hanke is a Johns Hopkins applied economist who is a specialist in currencies. His panacea for world economies suffering distress (that is a lack of confidence in the local money due to overprinting) is usually twofold, a currency board, where currencies are pegged to the dollar[9] or outright dollarization[10] of an economy. The only real difference between the two ideals is that the peg is fixed to a very specific number or percentile range and the nation-states central bank must keep dollars on hand to buy or sell into that peg as the local currency strengthens, or more likely, weakens. Whereas dollarization means the dollar becomes the real currency of that country, such as in tiny Ecuador or in Panama, or even Argentina, where the dollar, not peso trades as the de facto money. Hanke's advise to all Westphalian nation-states is the same prescription: use the dollar and your problems will go away. Unfortunately, this may not truly measure local economic conditions people face.

We discuss some types of well-known pegs and floats (quasi-pegs) here: The Hong Kong dollar (peg), Korean won, and Singapore dollar (dirty floats, where a currency's value is kept in a range). Even the Chinese yuan is pegged to a basket of currencies with its value determined daily by government apparatchiks, and not the market. The exact value of the Chinese basket is considered a "state secret" but is believed to be weighted greater than 60% in dollars. All countries measure the extent of their foreign reserve holdings in dollars. It is without saying that the major economies of the world then are not truly independent, but rather, "dollarized". The dollar is the all world currency. More on this and how that can be leveraged for change in particular with public goods problems is discussed in Chapter 10.

Already, the Hong Kong Monetary Authority (HKMA) has had to defend the Hong Kong dollar peg on a few occasions in recent years when speculative inflows or outflows tested the peg of HK$7.75 = $1 rate ceiling or at a HK$7.85 = $1 rate floor. The Singapore dollar trades in a "monitoring band", which is heavily skewed toward the US dollar, and administered by the Monetary Authority of Singapore (MAS) loosely set between S$1.20 and S$1.40 to one US$1 the past several years. A monitoring band is generally backed by a secret currency board, or basket of foreign currencies, say 70% in US dollars, 25% in euros, and 5% Australian dollars (the exact compositions are closely held by central banks and treasuries, and never publicized), whereby a trading band is linked to just one currency.

Until recently, due to the second financial crisis in 2008, QE (quantitative easing) and currency wars were back on in many countries around the world. The idea is that by a country weakening its currency significantly, it will spur economic activity exclusively by making its products and services cheaper to export than its neighbors thus stoking growth and jump-starting employment. The tool some countries use to do this is in printing more and more money. This practice started in Japan in 2001, but was popularized in 2008, under the then US Federal Reserve Chairman Ben Bernanke chiefly to address persistently high unemployment in the US labor markets. However, as the Economist pointed out about QE, "...*the flood of cash has encouraged reckless financial behaviour and directed a firehose of money to emerging economies that cannot manage* [i.e. not afford] *this...*". Consequently, today, a rapidly appreciating dollar is now causing havoc for many emerging economies, such as India, Indonesia, and Brazil, in ultimately paying back their dollar-denominated debts with localized earnings.

In other countries, such as big oil producers amidst falling oil prices, in Russia, Norway, and Venezuela, the markets can "force" a devaluation (or depreciation) through currency flight. Meaning foreign investment leaves and the local currency loses its collateral backing of hard currency reserves, held in a central bank, which have to be sold to temporarily maintain the local currency's value.

Holistically then, cheaper currencies mean cheaper labor costs, leading to cheaper exports, and overall lower costs of doing business domestically. This would be fine if countries operated singularly in economic silos, but they don't, they're interlinked with other country's economies. Additionally, it might be noted that elites in these countries usually don't keep their money in a local currency either, but rather in dollars and other foreign exchange. They have a huge advantage compared to the general populace when protecting their wealth. In this case, currency really does become a Westphalian game!

Weakening currencies though, for any reason, do carry real costs: to a country's citizens, especially if they have any reliance on imported foodstuffs, pharmaceuticals, energy, and technology. As most of these products, or their inputs are priced in dollars, the worlds "reference" currency. Consumers can experience ascending price shocks, sometimes on a daily level, such as in Argentina,[11] Venezuela, Zimbabwe,[12] or Ukraine. However, with social media and the Internet, central banks intentions can be amplified instantaneously to the markets. Making the stampede for dollars even more profound, as we saw in Turkey with people not trusting either the leader, Erdogan, or the Turkish lira.[13] The more he tells them things are fine, the more they gravitate to buying dollars. It becomes an ugly circular problem.

Recent events have shown that financial weakness and pending devaluations fool no one as they did before the advent of social media, pre-2000. It used to be the central bankers (the money managers of their respective Westphalian systems) who would announce currency devaluations late on Fridays, usually during a holiday weekend, after markets had closed, with citizens awakening on Tuesday or later, to find that their bank accounts had lost considerable real value. For example, with devaluation ongoing in Venezuela with the bolivar, and pending devaluation with the British exit of the EU or demonetization of certain denominations (500 and 1000 notes) in India, citizens have rushed to get their money out of bank accounts, and convert what holdings they have into dollars or other stable currencies, such as Swiss francs, Japanese yen, and euros. Simply, people around the world are no longer fooled by devaluations. Nationalist flag waving then becomes hollow when assets are involved. Information is disseminated immediately, and no one wants to be the last one arranging deckchairs on the proverbial Titanic.

Much of the pandemonium is driven by social media awareness and the viral internet, leading to larger macroeconomic ramifications in our interconnected world. If citizens can get their money out of the country before the devaluation occurs, then do these actions in and of themselves weaken monetary policy? For example, so many have pulled their money out of Russia or converted the ruble to dollars and euros, the rubles value plunged, from roughly 35 to $1 to approximately 67 to $1 in less than three months, even though Russia raised interbank lending rates to 17% at one point to compensate for the extreme devaluation, and said there would be no currency controls imposed at this time. Nevertheless, Russians were not convinced. Argentina has suffered a similar fate with its devalued peso, exacerbated with another default in July in 2014, and now perhaps a pending one in 2020. Argentina's exchange rate at the start of 2010 was peso 4 to $1, since then, it has soared to an official rate of ~ peso 60 to $1, As Argentines rely heavily on dollars for commercial transactions, a black market dollar market called the "*blue dollar*" has emerged, carrying nearly a fifteen-fold devaluation in less than a decade with peso borrowing rates pushed by the then Macri government to over 60%. Trust is obviously scant under Westphalian exclusivity.

Governments such as Venezuela have also tried to ease the rush to dollars by opening parallel exchange rates or creating new oil-backed cryptocurrencies. Nonetheless, these gimmicks have fooled no one. Long lines have formed as people cannot buy basic staples with imports that are prohibitively dollar costly. Foreign airlines operating in Venezuela face mounting losses on ticket sales and have suspended flights. The experiment with Chavez style economic Marxism, reliant on the price of one commodity, oil, has failed, leaving instead economic insecurity, street violence, extreme migration to regional nation-states, and food shortages. At the time of this writing, the US government is pushing hard for a regime change in Venezuela under the pretext of humanitarian concerns with the opposition leadership of Juan Guaido, and the Venezuelan bolivar is now essentially worthless at 250,000 to the dollar.

As we can see in Russia, Venezuela, and Argentina's cases, cheaper currencies have only brought misery due to declining living standards and soaring costs for dollar-priced imports. Central bankers have not been able to contain the damage as these situations are heavily subscribed to on social media such as Facebook, Twitter, WhatsApp, and various travel sites. These sites also recommend all types of remedies, schemes, and avoidances for citizens seeking to get their money out (or get dollars in at better rates), avoiding governmental currency controls and even fake money. We consider the story of Nigeria[14] and Egypt, two African economic giants who both rely on US dollars for their currency reserves but have approached devaluation in different ways. Egypt, by telegraphing the intent to devalue the pound far in advance, the other, Nigeria, by a creeping devaluation to bring the naira into alignment with a roaring black market. In both cases, telegraphing the decisions in advance, and attempted harmonization with the black market, only served to create a bigger frenzy for foreign exchange, that is dollars, earlier!

Conversely, the world of economic information has also created another demand: for safe havens. Traditionally, the US dollar has been the currency of choice, but past years of near-zero interest rates and now a $23 trillion public deficit have brough this into question, further the US has as much as $75 trillion in debt that will come due in the next 20 years.[15] People seek to put their "refugee-capital" into currencies backed by economies with strong balance sheets, high exports, small populations, and above all, social stability. Obviously, the Danish kroner, Japanese yen, and Swiss franc stand out among these, but they in turn, do not want hot money inflows that will make their currencies too expensive either. In times of uncertainty, these currencies can appreciate quickly. This happened in January 2016 in Switzerland, when the Swiss National Bank (SNB) lifted its euro cap (essentially a CHF 1.20 = €1 "ceiling peg") due to an increasingly weak euro[16] that appeared to be heading toward further weakness. It was an instinctive decision by the Swiss, but roiled world markets.

When the Swiss abolished the peg quite suddenly, within moments, the value of the franc had soared to 13.5% against the euro, wiping out many investor positions who were banking on a continually weakening franc due to the QE proclamations of EU Central Bank Chair Mario Draghi. The SNB had to scrap the peg as to continue buying a devaluing euro would not have made any economic sense. The SNB had to take this move secretly due to instantaneous communication. If it had been signaled beforehand, it could have benefitted some well-positioned actors more than others, creating a market bias, or as economists say "assymetric information". The games Westphalian financiers must go through to maintain or loosen values though demonstrate the amount of energy required to maintain the system and keep their own people in the dark.

A remedy in part for this is also maintaining a currency peg, to another, usually larger, trading partner. Hong Kong, as stated, pegs its dollar to the US dollar at a rate of 7.8 to $1, Denmark the kroner, to the euro at a rate of 7.45 to €1, and until recently, the Swiss franc had a ceiling against the euro of CHF1.20 to €1.

Further, the Swiss, Japanese, and Danish Central Banks have now imposed negative interest rates to stem the tide of those seeking haven for their money. This means that cash deposits on banks are charged yearly interest fees, of 0.50% in Denmark, and 0.75% in Switzerland. These countries adamantly do not want a tide of foreign money swamping their small economies and creating bloated exchange rates. We can see the Westphalian system is economically unforgiving.

REVALUATION: WHAT GOES DOWN ALSO GOES UP

So much has been written on the Chinese yuan currency it could fill a public library. Since China's opening up, the yuan has been on upward ascendency until August 2015, when it experienced a sudden devaluation due to a slowing Chinese economy, shaking world markets. This is a condition when a country adopts an exchange rate policy to boost its exports. China's exchange rate is representative of a managed float which is closely monitored and regulated by the Peoples Bank of China or PBOC. The yuan is predominantly anchored to the dollar and is allowed to move upward or downward around a 2% band set daily that is pegged to a dollar-weighted basket of currencies but on a sliding scale, that has recently been trending on the downslope, or "stealth devaluation" since 2016, to keep its exports competitive amidst a slowing economy with rising labor costs. Nonetheless people are not fooled. Chinese people want to get their money out to preserve their wealth. They want to buy foreign currency, stocks, or property and not be trapped inside the Chinese system only. The government knows this also, and China's typical Communist response has been to clamp down even harder on capital outflows, while talking about "eventually" revamping its export economy in very general terms, all the while floating even more government loans to its behemoth state-owned enterprises, where "reform" is an unknown term. What is key for China is preserving its Westphalian exclusivity and political stability at all costs, let the currency be damned.

It was Guido Mantega, the former Finance Minister of Brazil who in 2010 voiced his concern about an ongoing currency war of competitive devaluation practiced among trading partners. Setting the exchange rate closer to the market value is conducive for the competitive pricing of goods and commodities. China, Turkey, arguably South Korea, and some others are emerging upper middle-income economies transitioning away from the middle-income trap to a more developed economy status.

For countries faced with declining workforces and aging populations, it is understood that their economies are going to eventually slow down. There is then a strategic policy shift from an investment-driven economy to one guided by domestic consumption. It is therefore incumbent on the Westphalian state to stabilize the domestic economy before opening up its markets for any global investors. For China, which is centered toward pursuing and keeping in place, authoritarian capitalism, it is no doubt a challenging task to have a sustainable and workable blend of effective state control and the functioning of market forces of the invisible hand. Hence, in its economy which is trying to become a developed nation, there is a state-controlled exchange rate policy for achieving compatibility between social harmony and political stability. That is the theory that is being followed. People however, are skeptical of these changes in particular if it affects the value of their wealth.

Today, information of a currency's strengths and weakness is transferred instantaneously via the Internet and across social media. Central banks can no longer "surprise" the markets and take Draconian actions affecting both investors and ordinary citizens alike inside their sovereign exclusivity by secret decision. No nation has ever devalued its way to prosperity, nor, as in the case of Switzerland, can countries keep hot money inflows out if perceived as a safe-haven amidst a sea of volatility. Nonetheless, the Westphalian system is kept intact despite the fact that with social media, digitalization, and instantaneous economic communications, there can be no going back to the old days. Central bankers must create a better playbook that promotes public confidence instead of intrigue and confusion. Of course, this is a tall order, especially among elites who derive so much wealth from the current system of dollarization ascription against local currency devaluation.

THE BOND MARKET

The world then, in particular the developing world, as we start to see, runs on US dollars. That will not change anytime soon. Nowhere is this more mirrored than in the sovereign bond market (nation-states borrowing from foreign investors). The bond market is the most powerful financial interface in the world. In particular with the demand for US dollar denominated bonds, the *du jour* medium for borrowing for so many Westphalian projects, infrastructure, social, etc. Dollars account for most of the world's transactions. The bond market is held as sacred, and woe to any developing country that fails to honor its commitments to it. The country may delay, but eventually, it must pay, or be shunned by the international investment community. Meaning, it will not be able to borrow further in dollars, and lenders are usually not interested in dealing with local currencies, unless high interest rates are paid to incentivize them for greater risk taking. Both liquidity and stability are found in the dollar. That is the proof, that is played out in practicum.

Like the Chinese yuan, we could discuss the bond market also *ad nauseum*, but the key point is this: under Westphalia, money is paid in and out of its local transactions in domestic currency. For example, people in Turkey buy and sell in lira, and in Nigeria, naira, etc. That is all understood. But money is borrowed usually from the international markets in the form of dollar bonds, to finance projects, pay future bills, or cover social deficiencies. Simply because foreign investors do not trust the governmental meddling (exclusivity) in domestic currencies. The condition of course is that money borrowed in dollars must also be paid back in dollars. The problems arise when original leaders in those countries made promises of payback that future leaders or generations must honor on a timeline. If they default, their country will be punished severely by the markets. There is no escape. To shore up escaping these potential disasters, countries have gotten smarter to the fact that it is best to keep a large store of dollars in reserve, so their countries are never bankrupted again or held to the fire by foreign lenders (as is what happened in the Asian Crisis in 1997). This is especially notable in China, which at one point had a store of over $4 trillion, since then scaled back to $3.2 trillion to defend the value of its yuan currency. It must be emphasized the US dollar bond market and dollar bonds in general make up the majority of world financial transactions. In short, dollar bonds are the only game in town.

The point of both lessons in currency devaluation and bond issuance are that under Westphalia, people are aware of but rarely have a say in what their leaders and central banks are doing with their wealth. They seek alternatives and social media has enhanced this awareness, and allowed people to "vote with their feet" or currencies, but this has only led to a reactionary response from many countries to even impose further currency controls on the outflows of their currencies, or in allowing their money to be exchanged for foreign currency, albeit dollars. In other words, people cant get their money out of these countries. This then derives into another point, if the US dollar is the currency of choice for both foreign exchange reserves, and bond issuance, it effectively means the world becomes dollarized, and if Westphalia revolves around this, it can also be changed by it. Through all this we again note the determination of nation-states to preserve their largely dollar reserves.

Original Sin

In economic terms, original sin is any developing nation that over leverages its economy to an external foreign debt (again, mostly the US dollar) or essentially depending on another nation-states financial position to bolster its own aspects both due to a perception of global monetary stability and low, long-term interest rates. Economic scenarios generally not found in their own countries. With US dollar interest rates near zero for the past several years, dollar indebtedness has ballooned in so many developing countries. While better insulated from the effects of over-subscribing to another nation's currency these days, versus the financial crises of 1997, when so many Asian currencies fueled their economies in cheap dollars, developing countries are now holding larger amounts of foreign exchange (i.e. dollars). These countries receipts (payments) however are still derived in local currency, meaning any outflows of foreign currency still will be beholden to local exchange rates paid for that foreign currency, mostly the US dollar. For example, people in South America and Africa pay their electric bills and toll road fees in local currencies, however, the loans and bond covenants that were originally arranged to fund the power plant to provide the electric or the construction of that toll road were all paid for in dollar-backed bonds. This is the gist of the original sin argument. On the other side, one may argue that if not for loans of US dollars that power plant, airport, or road may have never been built in the first place.

The Trinity or the Impossible Dilemma

In principle, all Westphalian nations seek a currency then that can hold its strength freely, and whereas its central bank has a monetary policy free from foreign entanglements. However that requires hard work, patience, and (as we discussed in Chapter 5 about SOE's) significant economic restructuring. Oddly these are things the US also needs, as a purveyor of the dollar, but represents another story. Nonetheless, in the financial world today, only two of those given conditions of the following three are possible at any given moment.

1. A fixed foreign exchange rate (not dependent on another currency's value)
2. Free movement of capital across Westphalian borders (absence of capital controls)
3. An independent monetary policy (free from what other countries are doing, in particular the US Federal Reserve).

All the above conditions are in direct relation to the US dollar or the euphemistically called world "reserve currency". Most Westphalian nations today hitch their exchange rate or monetary policy (or both) to the dollar for stability because they simply could never meet all three conditions.[17] Some countries place capital controls on their money, meaning it is not easy to take the money out of their systems, and if so, generally finds few buyers abroad. A strong case of this is found in the Indian rupee. Not only is it difficult to take rupees out of India, but once out, no one is willing to buy them, if at all, unless heavily discounted. It this sense, the rupee is strictly an "inconvertible" currency, with value only to that nation-state. Any international projects involving foreign lenders would have to be in foreign currency, again, dollars, or they simply won't get done, but also subjecting India's citizens to the ultimate value of that foreign currency as future bills come due, against a perpetually devaluing rupee.

Understanding the Trinity is important as we will indicate later for this book's final recommendations about dealing with, and overcoming, Westphalia in a dollarized world. If the dollar is indeed the only game in town, then that sets the stage for new forms of governance that can create opportunities and win-win-win situations for many public goods problems we are faced with and no one wants to take ownership of.

Beyond the USD: A New Colonialism?

Dollar hegemony is simply here to stay. Other currencies either have too much internal political instability, like the euro, are too small, like the Swiss franc or pound sterling, or are not subject to market forces, like the PBOC controlled yuan. If one takes a step back, the US dollar also exhibits some of these problems, but as NYU economist Nouriel Roubini once said, "*the dollar is still the tallest midget in a roomful of midgets*". Practically, for Westphalia, it equates to neocolonialism via tethering to US economic policy for both the developing and extending to the upper middle-income world[18] where Venezuela,[19] Iran,[20] Egypt, Nigeria,[21] Turkey,[22] Indonesia, etc., economies are all based on dollars for energy, infrastructure, trade, and finance. A forced arrangement, similar to colonialism, whereby they have no choice but to continue using a "too big to fail" foreign currency.[23] All seeking to improve their economic lot against dollar goalposts, however there will be no new Plaza Accord[24] this time around, as it is not in elite interests to weaken the dollar further. As such, Westphalia allows developed country investors to continue to play off these countries by feeding them more and more dollarized debt, which they are addicted to. With no options on the horizon, and with these countries refusing to restructure, simply because politically they cannot, the band plays on. They become a prisoner of their own sovereign exclusivity game. Domestic currency valued outputs and payments, complete with dollarized inputs and obligations. While this chapter mentions many nation-states, the financial arguments all boil down to one nation-state in particular, the US, and how the world's dollar addiction for its perceived stability and store of value, despite all its theoretical flaws, only continues to grow. **The dollar has overshadowed Westphalia.** So we see that the system can actually be changed when value is at stake, similar to how Westphalia was originally conceived: the wealth of elites was at stake in times of great uncertainty. Perhaps to overcome Westphalia, fire must be fought with fire: the wealth of the elites must be at stake again.

The purpose of this chapter tells us two things in particular. First, the dollar is the all world currency that all other fiat currencies revolve around. Second, maintaining value under the exclusivity of the Westphalian system requires significant costs and sacrifices in relation to what other, nonexclusive currencies are doing. We will demonstrate the large implications this will have on confronting public goods problems on an enforcement level in Chapter 10. In short, Westphalia shows its overall ineffectiveness today when the real wealth of elites and nation-state is at stake.

Notes

1. God Speech (annotated) by Oscar nominated Ned Beatty from the 1976 movie *Network*.
2. Rothbard, M. (1961) What Is Money? pp. 82, 83. "At present, the world is enmeshed in a chaotic welter of exchange controls, currency blocs, restrictions on convertibility, and multiple systems of rates. In some countries a 'black market' in foreign exchange is legally encouraged to find out

the true rate, and multiple discriminatory rates are fixed for different types of transactions."

3. Das, S. (2016) Who Would Win a Currency War? No One. http://www. bloomberg.com/view/articles/2016-08-17/no-one-can-win-a-global-currency-war?cmpid=yhoo.headline&yptr=yahoo. Retrieved on February 2019.

4. Garber, P., and Spencer, M. (1994) The Dissolution of the Austro-Hungarian Empire: Lessons for Currency Reform. Princeton University: International Finance Section. http://www.princeton.edu/~ies/IES_Essays/E191.pdf.

5. Goodman, G. (1981) The German Hyperinflation, 1923. http://www.pbs.org/wgbh/commandingheights/shared/minitext/ess_germanhyperinflation.html. Retrieved on February 2019.

6. Bernholz, Peter, and Gersbach, Hans (1992) Gresham's Law: Theory. In *The New Palgrave Dictionary of Money and Finance*, vol. 2, 286–288. Macmillan: London and Basingstoke.

7. http://edition.cnn.com/2016/05/06/africa/zimbabwe-trillion-dollar-note/. Retrieved on February 2, 2019.

8. Funabashi, Yōichi (1989). *Managing the Dollar: From the Plaza to the Louvre*, 261–271. Peterson Institute. ISBN 9780881320978.

9. What Is a Currency Peg? (2016) *Business Insider*. http://www.businessinsider.co.id/what-is-a-currency-peg-20168/?r=US&IR=T#qUwt2MOoJ8zTvtjT.97. Retrieved on October 8, 2018.

10. DeFotis, D. (2017) 3 Venezuela Experts: Debt Risk & Dollar Adoption. *Barrons*. http://blogs.barrons.com/emergingmarketsdaily/2017/03/29/3-venezuela-experts-debt-risk-dollar-adoption/?ref=yfp. Retrieved on October 8, 2018.

11. DeFotis, D. (2015) 3 Shocking Stats From Argentina's 'Dirty' Currency Scheme. *Barrons*. http://blogs.barrons.com/emergingmarketsdaily/2015/12/17/3-shocking-stats-from-argentinas-dirty-currency-scheme/. Retrieved on October 9, 2019.

12. Cropley, E. (2017) Mugabe's Zimbabwe Gets Busy Creating 'Fiction Money'. *Reuters*. http://finance.yahoo.com/news/mugabes-zimbabwe-gets-busy-creating-140732720.html and http://fingfx.thomsonreuters.com/gfx/rngs/ZIMBABWE-DOLLARS/0100409Q0MV/index.html. Retrieved on September 30, 2018.

13. Aboufadel, L. (2018). Erdogan Tells Turks 'Change Dollars and euros to Lira'. *Almasdar News*. http://www.almasdarnews.com/article/erdogan-tells-turks-change-dollars-and-euros-to-lira/. Retrieved on October 8, 2018.

14. Agol, J. (2016) Nigeria's Naira Sinks in Free Float. Associated Free Press. http://www.yahoo.com/news/nigerias-naira-plunges-free-float-101418910.html. Retrieved on February 22, 2018.

15. Black, S. (2019) Four Ways That Uncle Sam Will Respond to Its $75 Trillion Insolvency. Sovereignman. http://www.sovereignman.com/trends/four-ways-that-uncle-sam-will-respond-to-its-75-trillion-insolvency-24879/. Retrieved on February 22, 2019.
16. Hickey, W. (2015) "Grexit" and Yuan Devaluation Could Put Significant Pressure on Asian Currency Pegs. Asia Development Institute Pathways Publication. http://www.asiapathways-adbi.org/2015/02/grexit-and-yuan-devaluation-could-put-significant-pressure-on-asian-currency-pegs/. Retrieved on February 21, 2019.
17. Patnaik, I., and Shah, A. (2010) Asia Confronts the Impossible Trinity (PDF). Working Paper 2010-64. New Delhi: National Institute of Public Finance and Policy.
18. Adinolfi, J. (2016) How Politics Rocked the Currency Market in 2016. Marketwatch.com. http://www.marketwatch.com/story/how-politics-rocked-the-currency-market-in-2016-2016-12-23?siteid=yhoof2&yptr=yahoo. Retrieved on February 22, 2019.
19. Editorial Board (2016) Venezuela Is Lurching Closer and Closer to Chaos. *Washington Post.* http://www.washingtonpost.com/opinions/global-opinions/venezuela-is-lurching-closer-and-closer-to-chaos/2016/12/26/63af5186-c79c-11e6-bf4b-2c064d32a4bf_story.html?ref=yfp&utm_term=.6760d0a21704. Retrieved on February 22, 2019.
20. Iran Rial Hits Fresh Record Low (2016) Associated Free Press. http://www.yahoo.com/news/iran-rial-hits-fresh-record-low-105648709.html. Retrieved on February 20, 2019.
21. Oyetunji, N. (2016). Why Dollar Rules Nigeria Read. Economic Confidential. http://economicconfidential.com/2016/04/dollar-rules-nigeria/. Retrieved on February 19, 2019.
22. Constantine, C. (2016). Turkish Lira Slips to Record Low on Fed Outlook; Bonds Decline. *Bloomberg.* http://www.bloomberg.com/news/articles/2016-10-28/turkish-lira-slips-to-record-low-on-fed-outlook-bonds-decline. Retrieved on February 22, 2019.
23. Fels, J. (2016) We Are Entering a 'Cold Currency War'. *Business Insider.* http://www.businessinsider.com/the-new-cold-currency-war-2016-12?IR=T&ref=yfp&r=US&IR=T. Retrieved on February 20, 2019.
24. No Secret Plaza Accord Deal to Devalue the Dollar (2016). http://www.afr.com/markets/no-secret-plaza-accord-deal-to-devalue-us-dollar-says-capital-20160320-gnmxi8. Retrieved on February 20, 2019.

CHAPTER 7

Westphalia in the Age of Social Media and Instant Communications

Social media is bending borders, it is largely uncontrollable outside of full censorship

Social media is simply put, the kryptonite to Westphalian exclusivity. In the seventeenth century media penetration and mobility was never envisioned. It was a world of coded messages and secrecy between elites. While Rene Descartes had published his *"I think, therefore I am"* contemporary to Westphalia in the mid-1600s, the age of enlightenment as expressed by the *Philisophes* was nearly 100 years away. The Guttenberg press while nearly 200 years old then, was still largely used to print religious works, its full media impact largely unknown. Today, the Internet and social media shines a clear and unambiguous spotlight on the doings of domestic governments, and allows them to be compared worldwide to what other governments are doing. Exclusivity is held up to the candle of transparency. Noble practices are feted, and lionized, such as quick responses to earthquakes and tidal waves. Ignoble purposes condemned, such as Friday night currency devaluations, cramdowns, extra-territorial incursions, and bail-ins, all in real time, with no reaction time for governments to respond. Social media is powerful, it now penetrates much of the world with large subscriber volumes. Think of Facebook, Twitter, WeChat, WhatsApp, Line, etc., mediums that spread instantly conversations and broadcast actions far and near. Actions of governments and their elites are quickly brought to light, so that hiding decisions or shirking responsibility is no longer possible. Media and social networks will find

© The Author(s) 2020
W. Hickey, *The Sovereignty Game*,
https://doi.org/10.1007/978-981-15-1888-1_7

you out, and you indeed will be found out. Westphalia can no longer assure the prized secrecy elites in control demand. Wikileaks, with its founder Julian Assange, has become the nefarious enemy of Westphalian secrecy.

Information has not only become instantaneous, but atomized. Board any bus, plane, or train, and people are automatically attenuated to their cell phones. They don't look at or talk to each other. This is atomized information. Information that is down to the individual's consumption, as opposed to TV or radio generated news or headlines. Considering today's average smartphone has the computing power of the entire Saturn V moon rocket Apollo program, this is indeed formidable. Of course most people while away this vast amount of empowerment watching Drake videos, K-pop harmonies, or Manchester United games, not realizing the truly informative power at their fingertips. This is similar to ducks, who can fly, but choose to waddle around instead. Most importantly, the internet is the conduit allowing information to flow freely across borders, how people ultimately use that information is the key to empowerment.

Near the time of the closing of writing this chapter, a lone gunman in Christchurch NZ, opened fired at a Mosque, killing 51 people and injuring scores. This horrific attack was "live streamed" online. It was instantaneously broadcast (going 'viral') worldwide, to over 60,000 onlookers on both Facebook and YouTube. These companies were also caught unaware and immediately took steps to scrub the Internet of its content related to them that they could control. It is an after the fact effort. While scrubbing the Internet will remove most content, anything downloaded or texted online spreads quickly and can remain there permanently. The shooter has gotten his point across using social media, the world cringes, but the dissemination of event and communication is instantaneous and difficult to control.

FISHING EXPEDITIONS

The power of the Internet and social media has conversely also given governments large scale access to the individual user's information and enabled the "surveillance state". How this information is used and for what purpose ultimately effects them. "Parallel Construction" essentially comes from big data fishing expeditions where users are noticed for a different transgression that was not part of the original search. This could be for many things, outstanding warrants, missed child support payments, most usually, back taxes or issues where taxes were missed in the first place, terrorist watch lists or for terrorism. Nonetheless under current rules and laws (in most Western countries), a pretext must be given in order to justify how the crime came about. Parallel construction essentially creates this framework, by the creation of a justification for the now known transgression. For example, thermal imaging allows police to monitor heat signatures. If they are looking for heat emitted by indoor marijuana growing, and stumble across a cache of illegal guns, the fishing expedition yielded a crime, but not the one originally suspected. Of course most of this borders on illegal searches and seizures, but big brother is desperate to justify a technology's use. Reasons must be given and many courts have interpreted parallel construction as a necessary loophole to preserve public safety.

However, a deeper issue than parallel construction is legal interpretation of control of the Internet. Will it truly be free or be regulated tightly by governments? The rules are still being sorted out and created daily. Regulations usually follow far behind technical innovations. Ideally, the rules should balance the individual's privacy with the power of government. Nonetheless, the government can be reactive not necessarily responsive to issues dealing with public safety or control. Consider that at first, Bitcoin was warmly received by many governments, including China, until they realized that a parallel currency (not parallel construction) could actually be a threat to their central banks if people were allowed to use an unregulated cryptocurrency instead of a fiat, controlled one.

What is reasonable, and how do governments determine public opinion? The effect of high technology on Westphalia is noted. Governments and elites seek to control their currency, public discourse, and trade tightly within their sovereign territory. Yet, social media, IT, and cryptocurrency are transborder. They can operate without the permission of a sovereign central authority. That is their appeal to the public, freedom from control. The only way that sovereign governments can control the pace is via the outputs inside their own domestic borders by blocking websites (China) or closing them off completely, banning cryptocurrency exchanges, limiting bandwidth (the US with the entire issue of internet freedom and commerce behind the guise of "net neutrality" where the Internet is wide open, but the speed of communications tightly controlled by for-profit companies). Nonetheless while the Internet and digital outputs are controlled, the cross-border activity goes on and increases exponentially.

So what will be the outcome of social media and Westphalian governance? Will it allow people to gain more individual power outside of their purview for communication, commerce, and information, or will it try to control the pace of technological absorption, using heavy-handed and ham-fisted tactics under the guise of public safety? To be sure, public safety is a legitimate concern in today's world, but the Westphalian system was never designed to deal with or encompass information technology or transparent communications in general, nor was it designed to deal with and remove 'fake news'. Westphalia is about exclusion and sovereignty inside a nation's borders, not about information sharing. Social media and the Internet are about creativity, freedom of expression, and cross-border communication. The two are seemingly but not necessarily on a collision course, with the old guard seeking to control while a younger group of technically savvy users wants open dialogue on a multitude of things. These questions will only grow in magnitude with criminal events being streamed to the world, but governments powerless to stop the progress of technology. Are we trying to poke fun at Westphalia? No, but the fact remains that in a world of digital media and instantaneous communications, governments must devise an inclusive information system of knowledge sharing, not in trying to withhold the truth behind an exclusivity arrangement that all can see through.

The key takeaway of this chapter is not an expose of all platforms of social media, but rather that the Westphalian entity can no longer neatly contain politically damaging information within its exclusive borders. The cat is out fhe bag. That is the theory, of course the reality is different and Westphalia is still blindly embraced.

BIBLIOGRAPHY

Descartes, R. (1637) Discours de la method. A Leyde (then publisher).
Yoo, J., and Philips, J. (2019) Technology and the Fourth Amendment, National Review (3/19).

CHAPTER 8

The Blockchain and Westphalia: Digitalization Crosses Borders

Today, technology allows individuals to communicate and transact freely without third-party interference or oversight. If decision-making can become apolitical and based on numbers, a new paradigm of objective governance can emerge, giving more power to the individual to create their own "store of value" and make decisions or influence the decision-making of others.

Bitcoin was an experiment by an unknown author (or authors) under the pseudonym Satoshi Nakamoto, in 2009 to create a digital currency based on data alone that would be free of the political entanglements and compromises that have plagued many of the world's socioeconomic systems, leading to economic reliance on mostly the fiat US dollar. In late 2017 this experimental "cryptocurrency" reached nearly $20,000 and many believed this would usher in a new world currency free from government interference and fiat. As of early 2020, the price of Bitcoin has since lost 50% off its highs, but a silver lining emerges in its core technology, the blockchain system behind it, which verifies all transactions by numbers and algorithms for data-driven decision-making, not politically compromised. This entire perspective could change the way business is done and governance administered, and in the process, enhance accountability and efficiency, minimizing corruption, or making corruption simply more costly to do.

© The Author(s) 2020
W. Hickey, *The Sovereignty Game*,
https://doi.org/10.1007/978-981-15-1888-1_8

The "blockchain" started as the decentralized IT system that under-pins cryptocurrencies. It offers a secure and impartial platform that can store vast amounts of transactions for any asset or item that can be digitized. Because it uses a methodology known as node consensus blockchain cannot be easily manipulated as it has a long history of transactions that promote continuity.[1] It cannot be hacked due to its long hash (#) codes, Merkle trees, and legacy of transactions that promote continuity of any object by node consensus (that means agreement of the majority of users). A node is simply any person behind a terminal that has access to any particular blockchain. This means the blockchain ultimately has the potential to eliminate any and all bureaucracy involved in governance. This is of particular importance for developing countries with politically placed and top-heavy bureaucracy, and usually with a history of corruption. The key to incorporating the blockchain in systems is not solely in its IT proficiency, which has been extensively documented[2] but in gaining acceptance from key policymakers, leaders, and elites whose roles become redundant under the blockchain's most optimal utilization: trust. Change is not easy.

The core idea behind the blockchain is simply to get computers using energy to prove that they are trustworthy, and time stamping that "trust" on the "blocks" of all the recorded transactions digitally. This then becomes the blockchain, with data stamped immutably on the system, meaning it could not be politically overridden or hacked easily as the vast data underpinning each decision to encode that data is overseen by all nodes on the network. One could theoretically still lie to the network, but they would need to burn more energy doing so than perhaps any honest participant, combined, by creating essentially veracity behind the new equations, defined on blockchain as "proof of work" in reaching a consensus of participants (or computer terminals as nodes).

In conjunction, Bitcoin, which is based on the blockchain, was an experiment to create digital peer-to-peer (P2P) transactions, devoid of political interference or third-party oversight.[3] The endeavor attempted to avoid governmental compromises that have plagued many of the world's socioeconomic systems due to the power of Westphalian fiat currencies. Bitcoin, with the blockchain system behind it, verifies all transactions by numbers and algorithms for data-driven decision-making, making it devoid of politics. This changes the way business is done and governance administered, enhancing accountability, efficiency, and minimizing corruption by making it simply too costly to engage in.

What Is the Blockchain?

The blockchain is an evolution of the "Big Three Exponentials" from the past 50 years of the information revolution: computing (the PC: *Moores Law*, or doubling of computing power every five years), communication (the Internet: *Butters Law*, or the doubling of transmission every nine months), and now, data storage (the blockchain: *Kryder's Law*, whereby storage of data becomes cheaper and cheaper). The blockchain stores data not only in gigabytes, but in terrabytes, that is *thousands* of gigabytes. It is truly a formidable design.

The blockchain is a chain of blocks where information in code is recorded. When these blocks are chained together, the perfect audit history is created. One can go back in time and see any former state of the database, at a specific time stamp, anytime. If recording things like property titles, one can see all previous owners of the property (provided they were recorded) and the current owner. There is simply no ambiguity.

Blockchain, the IT protocol, or language, that underpins Bitcoin and other cryptocurrency, is a distributed ledger, or database, that is shared across a computing network. Each computer terminal that a person sits behind, or "node" in the network, holds a copy of that ledger, making the blockchain extremely data storage intensive but insuring there is no single point of failure. True to its namesake, every piece of information is mathematically encrypted and added as a new "block" to a chain of historical records. Various consensus protocols, meaning agreement with all the other nodes, are used to validate a new block with updated information before it can be added to the chain (Fig. 8.1).

Each block consists of data related to a specific transaction. The **hashes** (#'s) in each block are the long numerical/alphabetical code particular to the transaction detail, the **text root** includes all pertinent details of that transaction in the block, a *nonce* is a signature that can be used only one time in a *cryptographic* communication, it is issued as an authentication protocol to ensure that old communications cannot be used again. The timestamp precisely records when the transaction happened. Importantly, the transaction's time and occurrence become "immutable", they cannot be changed or manipulated at a later date and could not be overridden or hacked easily as the vast data underpinning each decision to encode that data is overseen by all nodes on the network.

The blocks together create a perfect audit history of transactions. One can go back and see a former state of the database at any point in time. If recording things like property titles, one can see all previous owners of the property (provided they were previously recorded) up to the current owner.

The schematic of the blockchain

Proof of work consensus on the blockchain (Source: Peck, as adapted by Hickey)

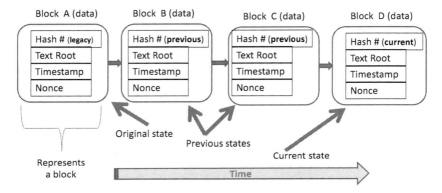

Fig. 8.1 The blockchain schematic (*Source* Adapted from spectrum. ieee.org [Peck, M. (2015) The Future of the Web Looks a Lot Like the Bitcoin Blockchain. http://spectrum.ieee.org/computing/networks/the-future-of-the-web-looks-a-lot-like-bitcoin. Retrieved on January 31, 2019] [by W. Hickey])

All this is critical to the independence of the system. The blockchain can give data the continuity of real-world assets. Any asset that can be digitized can be placed on the blockchain: a certificate, deed, bank statement, spreadsheet, diploma, etc. Continuity is a universal precept of the physical world. Legal and political systems are based on assumed continuity of assets, in other words, establishing a paper trail. Namely, the identity of things with the people that go along with them. The entire world legal and political system is based on the continuity of assets. Namely, the identity of things with the people that go with them. That being, certifications, passports, licenses, notaries, stamps, government-issued identifications, titles. Without continuity, there is no P2P and there can be no foundation for an identity, proof of ownership, involvement in transactions, creation of trust, or contractual obligations. Intermediaries such as governments, banks, and insurers are the traditionally accepted parties, rooted in historical precedence, that step into create continuity.

This continuity of transactions then forms an encrypted "chain" of specific numbers demarcated with a hashtag (#) to create veracity by a majority of participants who accept them by workload consensus. This continuity of data becomes to make the virtual world...*real*.

The blockchain disrupts this tradition. Its continuity of transactions forms an encrypted "chain" of numbers to create veracity by the majority. Simply, any political decision can be complemented by the truth of numbers, and not influenced by subjective compromises. We consider an operations management perspective here. If losses from poor transactions can be limited, business (and governance) becomes more efficient as time-consuming transactional frictions that limit capacity are removed. These frictions and inefficiencies also represent non-intended opportunities from petty theft and pilferage to the large scale corruption and rent-seeking activities of government officials and elite insiders. This is referred to as a "DAO system" or decentralized autonomous organization, which means the automation of governance and decision-making. It must be noted, however, that the entire concept of DAO and its legality is a highly contentious governance issue.[4] Continuity of data can make all digitized things pertaining to physical documents suffice without the need of any physical repository. The blockchain then has the potential to be a very "disruptive technology" to traditional governance.[5] The blockchain's clear and unambiguous record cannot be corrupted or changed later. Further, the macro implications of the blockchain limiting corruption will have bigger implications on megaprojects, such as refineries, nuclear power plants, and dams that must come in on budget and other large government initiatives such as economic development and poverty alleviation.

If transactions can be rooted and underpinned outside of physical accounting books and government file cabinets which are overseen by bureaucrats who can be compromised, and instead embedded in mathematical and algorithmic data, unbiased veracity of all transactions could be assured. This means opportunities for corruption could also be limited, which would be extremely valuable in the further national economic development for developing countries, such as African countries along China's Belt and Road Initiative (BRI), or with oil and gas project development in central Asia, or with infrastructure projects in South America. The latter two examples, historically plagued with corruption. Much of blockchains utility and potential then fit more suitably in emerging economies, as opposed to developed ones with a legacy of regulations and robust, long time institutions already in place.

This is not to say that the blockchain is not without some serious technical limitations by any means, however. First, it is an electricity hog, making it environmentally destructive, which is particularly problematic for electric poor developing nations where it can be of the most use. Second, it has huge digital storage needs, as mentioned, in terrabytes. Third, it can only process so many transactions per minute, all the required data storage and constant updating is a very slow process. Thus, beyond its political acceptance, the other problem facing the blockchain is its scalability. It must be able to grow to meet the demand for many transactions in a less energy-intensive format. Blockchain also has one major practical limitation: it is only as good as the initial inputting. As a system, it does not ensure the quality of the inputted data. If a fake record is recorded and inputted as real, it will stay on the system, and trying to change that later will result in having to create another chain of nodal consensus, there is no way to overwrite. Note that a consensus of users would be required to accept the fake record from the beginning, so this theoretically limits this risk.

THE BLOCKCHAIN AND PEER-TO-PEER (P2P) PLATFORMS

This consensus then creates veracity, or trust, between the two parties engaging in transactions, or P2P. The identities of these parties on the network can be established definitively via their exclusive digital "signatures", and in turn, these individuals can sign and verify transactions themselves. As such, if the integrity of the data is ensured between two participants, there is no need for a third party such as a bank or government office to officiate and referee the transaction, the consensus mechanism of the nodes on the blockchain assumes this mantle. Known as disintermediation, it is one of the ways blockchain creates value and lowers costs by having no centralized authority.[6] Consider an example: the UN, delivering some of their aid to war-torn Syria, has used a blockchain-based distribution solution. By so doing this, they can authenticate individuals using biometric data to ensure that the aid is given to the right people in an equitable quantity, reducing leakage to any imposed "fee's" and commissions; in particular to rent-seeking officials. The reality however faces challenges of control, be it arbitrary or legitimate, from political leaders and human systems which can have very vested interests. The blockchain presents an opportunity to reforming these systems that vast economic and development programs have not been able to achieve. Also, in eliminating the *System D* (world shadow) economy of the unbankable, estimated to be at $10 trillion, by bringing in more people to share on P2P platforms rather than in using high-cost intermediaries or paying for red tape they cant afford.

For example, consider what blockchain can potentially do for land ownership and transfers. We live on an overpopulated planet of 7.2 billion people. Arable land is a finite scarcity and a historical family legacy for many. However, proving clear title and ownership to the land becomes a business in itself, particularly in developing countries in South Asia and Africa. In some cases, officials or politicians in countries with weak legal rights will carefully observe unclaimed or unaccounted land over time. Then, when opportunity arises, they will adjust books, deeds, and unclear titles to usurp it for themselves. Additionally, transferring land, or any scarce resource, becomes an opportunity for all types of bureaucracy to insert themselves: tax officials, notaries, surveyors, environmental authorities, and others. This results in tremendously slowing down the process or making it outright impossible for the poor to transfer land or prove ownership. See Fig. 8.2.

If transactions can be rooted and underpinned outside of physical accounting books and government file cabinets which are overseen by people who can be politically compromised, and instead embedded in

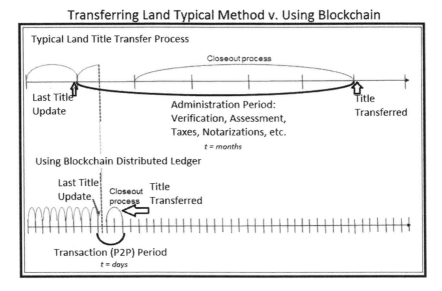

Fig. 8.2   For the typical property title transfer, versus ideal property transfer on the blockchain (Hickey)

mathematical and algorithmic data, unbiased veracity of all transactions (registration, payments, insurance, and ticketing) could be assured. If the blockchain is adopted as the sole source of documentation authenticity, opportunities for corruption or political compromise become limited. In developing countries where economic development projects continue to be a daily reality this is extremely valuable. For example, the blockchain would give a large company such as DeBeers, who presumably can be held accountable by the public, a real way to ensure that the diamonds in its supply chain were not mined in conflict areas using forced and child labor. Today, blood diamonds are laundered into the system by paying off customs officials and border guards to make them appear as if they were mined somewhere else. The encrypted blockchain database allows only those with permission—from mining to cutting to selling—to record the diamond's journey (or provenance) on the immutable record.[7] Anyone then involved in future transactions can go to the blockchain ledger and seek the entire history of that particular item.

The blockchain is already undergoing furious application development in a variety of other contexts[8] and platforms, while financial technology or "Fintech" is the predominant economic driver (due to the cashed-up interests driving it), blockchain usage now encompasses food security, diamond registry, logistics, and music/artistic creation, but its most useful application and biggest potential is yet to be seen: underpinning governance as a neutral and uncompromised data verification system.

A Deeper Introspect for Governance

To clarify, any governance entity, whether—democratic, authoritarian, theocratic, or other type, such as a political union, is a body which (successfully or unsuccessfully) claims a monopoly on violence over a specific territorial area, and in return this entity is expected to provide various degrees of government services such as police and military, dispute resolution, and civil enforcement for their citizens.[9] Thus said, if contracts, land registry, social insurance, taxes, voter identification, education and census records can be placed on the blockchain and accepted legally as a valid medium of recognition, much bureaucratic meddling, inefficiency, and opportunities for corruption could be mitigated. A new system has emerged. History has shown however, that when entrenched interests are threatened, in particular economic interests, violence, and reprisal are assured reactions. If it cannot be controlled, it becomes an existential threat, and will be treated as such. In this case, it will be the veracity of the blockchain, against the many interpretations of truth by people, namely, people in power.

Compounding rights and other governance issues is the fact that nation-state borders continue to represent oppression to millions in a digital age of atomized information in mostly the undeveloped world. For example, oil and gas can flow freely *under* borders, but a human cannot go freely *over* them. The tensions created by arbitrarily drawn state borders are perhaps exemplified by both the Berlin Conference of 1885, and thirty years later, the Sykes–Picot agreement in 1916. In the former, African borders were arbitrarily drawn by European powers (with no Africans present) under a German king, to satisfy a craving for territorial hegemony[10]; in the latter, during the waning years of the ailing Ottoman Empire, Middle-Eastern borders were crudely drawn pursuant to European colonial interests of that period. Both have exacerbated ethnic and religious conflict to this day with fighting and disagreement. It is noted that attempts to redraw borders in Africa or the Middle East based on ethnic and tribal identity has largely failed, only to be met with war, as the Westphalian system gained root quickly and became intoxicating, forever empowering a new elite base in each country that had no incentives to return to former ways or allegiances.

Blockchain technology, in tandem with the previously mentioned "three exponentials" now enables for the first time a way to verify all transactions without a single authoritative third party sitting in between, and may now be the best time in recorded history to revisit and question reliance on the traditional Westphalian nation-state, formatted over 350 years ago, as an outdated governance system which is blocking human social and economic evolution and discourse.[11] This matters greatly as a blockchain transactional database can maintain the basic record-keeping properties required in and for any governance system.

Rather, governments themselves should drive transformative blockchain applications in identity cards, health care, and digital currency for needed system updates. They have the incentive and the critical mass, especially in developing countries, to be receptive to blockchain technology. Unfortunately, the technological penetration in the developing world still remains low and is a major educational challenge.

IMPLICATIONS

The blockchain then is not merely about a new type of computer code for accounting. It is also a fundamental shift in thinking away from the purely physical realm of transactions to creating a virtual realm where interactions between parties are based on the trust in encrypted data, without the need of a third party inserting themself for verification, whether governmental or private.

In order for the blockchain to be most effective and useful for society, it has to first overcome its political acceptance problems, and secondly, its scalability problems. Those things said, the blockchain is real and has a data-driven societal transformative potential to create unbiased and uncompromised record-keeping that cannot be easily accomplished through political dialogue alone.

The implications for governance are vast. In the short term, this means a better way for countries to manage their internal bureaucratic processes as well as pressing global issues, climate change, plastic waste, immigration, and megaprojects. Public goods issues that are digitized will be easier to identify the actors and causes. But in the long term, blockchain's anonymous cross-border functionality challenges the traditional nation-state as an organizing method for people. Westphalia has unwanted digital competition if may not easily embrace!

SUMMARY

A blockchain then is really a method for any data or information from its incipiency to be stored electronically and distributed across an entire user based network for public disclosure. This information is therefore transparent for any transaction on a given ledger past and current, with identifiable time stamp along the way. Government data is usually siloed in bureaucratic offices and can be non-transparent. The blockchain can serve to simplify citizen's interactions and access to this information.

The blockchain is a fundamental shift in thinking away from the purely physical realm of transactions (public and private) previously conducted under the watchful gaze of government officials, lawyers, and bankers, to creating a virtual realm where an interaction can be completed between two parties only with the same trust underpinned by encrypted data that ensures asset continuity. In other words, the technology is there to create an entirely new world of governance, but is the political will?

Notes

1. What Is a Node? » Learn About Blockchain Tech | Lisk Academy. Lisk. http://lisk.io/academy/blockchain-basics/how-does-blockchain-work/nodes. Retrieved on February 7, 2019.
2. The Promise of the Blockchain: The Trust Machine. *Economist*, October 31, 2015, economist.com and Federal Reserve Bank of St. Louis *Review*, First Quarter 2018, 100 (1): 1–16. http://doi.org/10.20955/r.2018.1-16.
3. Satoshi, N. (2008) Bitcoin: A Peer-to-Peer Electronic Cash System. http://bitcoin.org/bitcoin.pdf. Retrieved on March 12, 2018.
4. Jentzsch, C. (2016) Decentralized Autonomous Organization to Automate Governance. Kiron, D. et al. (2016) Aligning the Organization for Its Digital Future. *MIT Sloan Management Review* 58 (1).
5. Limsanarphun, N. (2018) SEAC to Guide Managements Through Disruptive Digital Transformation. http://www.nationmultimedia.com/detail/Economy/30335526. Retrieved on March 12, 2018.
6. Hern, A. (2016) Blockchain: The Answer to Life, the Universe and Everything? http://www.theguardian.com/world/2016/jul/07/blockchain-answer-life-universe-everything-bitcoin-technology. Retrieved on March 12, 2018.
7. Marr, B. (2018) How Blockchain Could End the Trade in Blood Diamonds. http://www.forbes.com/sites/bernardmarr/2018/03/14/how-blockchain-could-end-the-trade-in-blood-diamonds-an-incredible-use-case-everyone-should-read/#5b76eebe387d. Retrieved on February 16, 2019.
8. Fingas, J. (2018) Coca-Cola and US Government Use Blockchain to Curb Forced Labor. http://www.yahoo.com/news/coca-cola-us-government-blockchain-163200292.html. Retrieved on March 12, 2018.
9. North, D. (1990) *Institutions, Institutional Change and Economic Performance*. UK: Cambridge University Press.
10. DW. (2015) 130 Years Ago: Carving Up Africa in Berlin. http://www.dw.com/en/130-years-ago-carving-up-africa-in-berlin/a-18278894. Retrieved on January 2, 2019.
11. Philips, A. (2016) Why the Peace Treaty of 1648 Merits Scrutiny Today. http://www.thenational.ae/opinion/why-the-peace-treaty-of-1648-merits-scrutiny-today-1.203678. Retrieved on March 18, 2018.

CHAPTER 9

Tax Policy and Westphalia

Misguided Taxation Policies Wreak Havoc in the Westphalian World

National economic competitiveness and rising GDP's are generally not induced by people paying more taxes, but less, ala Hong Kong, Chile, Singapore, and Switzerland are all highly productive economies. The high tax exceptions to this would be Germany and the UK with developed economic systems, transparency, ease of doing business, and limited state intervention in industry. Recently, and in tandem with the Organization for Economic Cooperation and Development (OECD) and IMF, developing countries have been pushing to increase tax collection in their home countries, such as Indonesia, Brazil, India, and South Africa, without addressing the fundamental structural issues that have become a long part of their modern, and usually postcolonial, histories, no doubt due to pressure from the same Washington/Brussels consensus that has trained them, but ignores on the ground realities.

Tax amnesties and GSTs (General Services Taxes) designed to "shake the money tree" of their populations in order to pay for ever-increasing public debts, bureacracy, and costly obligations such as pensions and energy subsidies are being applied as a way to "equitably solve" revenue shortfalls. Nonetheless, chasing low-income citizens around for marginal taxes while not addressing causations embedded in the structures of their societies will not equalize this.

For example, Prime Minister Narendra Modi's India is too complex economically to apply a Western-style GST overnight. Its patchwork of many local and state taxes cannot be overridden as simply as removing from circulation high-value Indian rupee notes, nonetheless it is the first start toward a tax harmonization policy.

Indonesia, the world's fourth largest country, is towing the IMF/OECD line for tax amnesties and information sharing, yet results have been poor. Further, with significant corruption issues still unresolved, and without strict protocols in place, OECD adherent countries may not have to reciprocate the same tax information anticipated. So many have avoided Brazil's amnesty (RERCT) that it has been extended an additional four months due to lack of interest. Essentially, people don't trust their Westphalian governments, in particular in developing countries. No amount of pressure from rich Western countries or their supranational institutions, like the IMF or OECD, can change that.

The EU-centric OECD based in Paris, Agreement on Exchange of Information on Tax Matters (AEOI) and the US implemented FATCA are developed country mechanisms for *their* tax problems that simply cannot be applied easily to developing countries with the underlying economic growth problems of workforce modernization, endemic corruption, and overly bearing regulations left unresolved. China interestingly has, similarly to the US, since 1990 sought global taxation of all its citizens and residents, as does Indonesia, but both lack the dollar currency to enforce transactions globally, which only the US can clearly monitor through its exchanges.

These three issues: equitable tax collection, tax amnesties, and enforcement, preclude the objective and transparent governance required for effective tax collection in order to spur economic growth. For political reasons, namely a deep recalcitrance to change their domestic economic structures which, again, falls under the Westphalian rubric of "exclusivity", these issues are almost as robust today as they were 20 years ago, and even before the first Asian economic crisis in 1997.

Structural Reforms

These are the "heavy-lifting" reforms needed to make economies more competitive, namely, reducing nation-state guarantees for employment, entitlements, and pensions, and reducing industrial support in the form of SOEs (state-owned enterprises) which require massive cash infusions to run, and as stated in Chapter 5.

This is a complicated situation where China is the world's poster boy of SOEs due to the enormous amount of industries that are being subsidized and protected by the government to insulate unskilled and redundant workers from being laid off or fired. Nonetheless, many other countries also have behemoth SOEs, mostly in fossil fuels and infrastructure companies (construction, railways, utilities, etc.), that employ millions of redundant and unnecessary workers simply to keep political stability, and are isolated from international competitive factors. Increasing tax collection to pay for these ongoing domestic monopoly situations only serves to hinder, not promote, the necessary economic competitiveness sorely needed on an overcrowded planet.

CORRUPTION

The trust issue is however the largest impediment to enacting modern taxation regimes in the developing world. One taxation theory holds that people don't pay taxes in developing economies, as they don't see the money being used for civil society, but rather for the purposes of elite insiders, in particular for vanity projects: fountains, stadiums, statues, etc. A perpetual (and justified) distrust of leaders exists due to this wasteful and non-transparent spending. In this case, a very different paradigm from the European OECD expectation model countries of government accountability emerges. Trust takes a long time to build but can be shattered instantly. For example, citizens in Malaysia and Brazil are asked to take part in transparent tax amnesties, disclosing *their* life savings, despite the ongoing political corruption scandals in the billions of dollars with MDB 1 in the former, and the Petrobras 'car wash' scandal in the latter. Both scandals ensnared gigantic state-owned enterprises with direct connections to these nation's leaders and their coterie. Citizens then have concerns that tax amnesties under corrupt officials can become fishing expeditions to settle political scores and not about developing civil society or improving their lives. There is a legitimate trust concern with these issues. We can also see how people in the digital age become trapped in their Westphalian prisons, forced to pay for their nation-state's incompetence, waste, or authoritarianism when comparable nation-states enact more realistic and fair regimes. As stated in Chapter 7, social media and the Internet underpin the awareness factor today.

Nonetheless, leaders still blindly feel that dollar-based Western-style economic solutions will strengthen their economic activity and tax revenue enhancement if they can only be enacted. One need look no further than Greece, an EU member and the historic founder of Democracy, to see that if Greek distrust of tax collection in its current guise is so problematic, how much moreso in developing countries, without traditions of egalitarianism and under top-down, unelected, authoritarian leadership? In sum, taxes are not just about collecting money, but also a reflection of the society's trust and transparency in their financial systems.

By contrast, Argentina's tax amnesty has been a relative success, bringing in over $117 billion with a then leadership that was considered progressive and market friendly. Despite political upheavals, Argentina, until the turn of the millennium was generally considered the most developed country in all of Latin America, with the highest incomes. In other words, the institutions and development indexes in Argentina are closer to Scandinavia than Southeast Asia. Meaning, despite their current problems, some faith has been placed in Argentine institutions. Nonetheless, investors and citizens have been burned before by Argentine politicians, so again, trust looms as a major factor. The very recent election of a new Peronist government in 2019 has revived these trust anxieties.

Overbearing Regulations

This is about overhauling the legal system, in order to promote better privately owned business, in particular small and medium-sized enterprises (SMEs) that are tightly controlled in many developing countries so as not to challenge the political influence of behemoth SOEs in critical, and lucrative industry, such as banking, insurance, transportation, telecom, and energy. Which harkens back to our opening point, structural reforms. Developing countries all tend to overregulate the mundane issues such as multilayered regulations, permissions, and zoning plans, while underregulating the more serious ones, such as youth smoking, highway and food safety, and labor laws. These regulations drive up costs and investors look elsewhere.

The bottom line here is that merely implementing tax collection practices, such as GSTs, VATs, amnesties, and information exchanges, does nothing in itself to address the three main issues of structural reform, regulatory issues, and corruption deficiencies in emerging economies, though it makes great press and establishes bogeymen for financial ministries to pursue. Further, these tax mechanisms and reporting standards were largely created for the benefit of wealthy Western countries with numerous institutional safeguards and reforms in place, not developing ones that refuse to deal with their political issues for stability. We demonstrate that a clear imbalance among Westphalian states exists that has been laid bare by social media and the Internet, with glowering contradictions and fueling peoples distrust.

International institutions such as the OECD, World Bank, and IMF and monetary officials such as central bankers and financial ministers trained in developed Western countries can no longer promote (or dictate) the localized trust necessary to form the social-capital bond that ensures transparency, promotes trust, creates legal certainty, and reduces cronyism. Taxation avoidance then is a symptom of all these underlying issues, and is not the core problem. In other words, there is a reason to the method.

IDEAL TAXATION ACROSS ALL WESTPHALIA

It can be deducted then that the unevenness of Westphalia promotes push and pull factors between sovereign nations, in particular developed and developing, that cannot be easily reconciled and creates financial imbalances. People and companies will continuously flee to lower tax areas if they believe their money will be squandered or given over to corruption and of which they have no voice in the matter. Taxes policy in Congo with a long history of perfidy and corruption is not of the same standard as tax policy in Canada, which has robust institutions in place to check and balance the system. No amount of well-wishing by supranational institutions like the IMF or World Bank can convince people that all states are equal. Perhaps it is best to discuss an ideal taxation regime that is based more on social capital and less on enforcement under the guise of nation-state "exclusivity". If we consider the Scandinavian countries (Denmark, Sweden, Iceland, and Norway) with some of the highest tax rates in the world (>50% on incomes) inequality and corruption are very low.[1] We could consider this an ideal. People there do not overly complain about taxes (and tend to be shocked by people who do) as they can witness what actually becomes of their money, and how they benefit personally, unlike other countries with lower tax rates, but considerably less government transparency and services. Consider the evidence:

Education is generally free, and for all strata of the society. Students are not hamstrung to a life of student debt or taught a regime of political nonsense. Living costs for students are also subsidized by the state, and payback is a low interest rate tied to the ability to repay.

Childcare is also subsidized by the state, so people are not tempted to hire illegal migrants to mind them, or have to work two jobs. Maternal and paternal leave is paid by the state.

Universal healthcare is a given. It is directly financed by taxes, and deductibles are capped at low levels compared to the US. There are never any issues regarding preexisting conditions. It is full coverage for all. Yes, the healthcare may not be the most innovative for the very sick, as can be given in a profit driven US system, but the safety net covers all, with few falling between the cracks or left uncovered.

The social programs that are in Scandinavia are more generous than other countries. Unemployment benefits can cover one for up to 2 years. If people get sick, they can stay at home with full pay. This also applies to children, if they get ill, a parent will receive full pay to stay at home and care for them.

Government and public services are run quite efficiently. Corruption is so rare, that most feel sure their tax money will go to the purpose it is intended for. International military excursions, a military industrial complex, and large vanity projects are avoided. Infrastructure is built, roads, bridges, airports are all visible outcomes. Clean water is taken for granted. Electric is reliable, with blackouts largely nonexistent. Things work, and life can be enjoyed. Safety and police protection is unbiased and reliable. Of course this is all the ideal!

The point of this chapter, is that overall, even though taxes in Scandinavia are high, the outcomes and distribution of where their taxes go are very visible. Of course Scandinavia is bulwarked by centuries-old institutions with small, homogenous populations that are of similar culture. Nonetheless, this of course sets the ideal for an interconnected world and a template which highlights national decisions regarding how taxes and public expenditures could be, many now wonder why can't their taxes also be used in a similar way? People in our interconnected world simply are not sold that they must be funding foreign wars, vanity projects, endless entitlements, and government incompetence, that are force-fed to them under the Westphalia's exclusivity arrangement, and they certainly do not want to be co-opted into it forever. All taxpayers today demand choice, accountability, and results for their money. Instead of chasing other Westphalian nation-states for an "exchange of information", or ways to implement various GSTs, sales taxes, tariffs, transfer pricing arrangements (where international businesses shop for the lowest tax Westphalian state to book profits), and value-added taxes, it may work for the better to encourage a gainsharing device among people that is visible, so they wouldn't want to avoid taxes in the first place. While Westphalia allows opt-outs, it also allows "opt-ins". Opting into a system like Scandinavia has would bring more tax compliance and less avoidance. Unfortunately,

Scandinavia is a very tiny part of the world with longstanding egalitarian traditions, homogeneity, and shared traditions/ethnicity/language, many much older than Westphalia itself. Westphalia however, left to itself, only continues to pit nation-states against each other with its mandate of sovereign exclusivity.

FATCA and AEOI

The US dollar is a de facto bankrupt currency. No other nation in the world could hold a $22 trillion (and growing) national debt and stay financially solvent. It is only because the dollar is the world's reserve currency (Chapter 6) buoyed by a global perception and confidence in its value that this can keep going on, seemingly defying all economic laws. Nonetheless, the US must have worldwide receipts to keep this economic show going particularly in regard to its domestic entitlements (social payments) and being the world's policeman (US President Donald Trump has proposed a 2019 military budget of $750 billion, a mind-boggling sum). Similarly, the big European economies are also dead, the cradle to grave welfare system and slowing growth have long hobbled their economies. They also badly need new revenue streams. The elites also know this, and tend to put their money out of the hands of the places tax collectors go by placing it in other sovereign, Westphalian entities. *They* do not want *their wealth* absconded by governments that will not and cannot restructure their systems. Additionally, with world mobility, many Americans and Europeans do not live in their home countries anymore. They have taken up residence in other Westphalian lands, in particular developing countries, such as Malaysia, Thailand, Tunisia, Costa Rica, Panama, etc., where living costs are substantially lower and the prying eyes of Westphalian governance more subdued.

Nonetheless, both the US and EU countries want to get their hands on income and revenue parked by those holding their passports but living in other countries, so they have derived extra-territorial tax systems to force compliance. In the case of the US, the FATCA (Foreign Account Tax Compliance Act) law was created in 2010. The US (and everyone else) knows that the world runs primarily on the dollar. The law forces any bank that deals in dollars (and most do to maintain their business competitiveness) to report on US citizens and residents who keep their money there under threat of being frozen out of this dollar system.

As banks do not want to lose access to their lifeblood currency, they essentially become arms of the US Internal Revenue Service. We will come back to this issue of dollar usage in this chapter. It is such a powerful currency, that no country or bank wants to be cut off from it. We note that the Westphalian allegiance and kowtowing (national pride) is quickly swept aside when foreign exchange or hard currency is involved! As a further note, FATCA does not assure any reciprocity with the other nations it coerces. It is a one-way agreement, which benefits the US and dollar receipts, and compliance is forced under duress of being cut out of the world's financial system.

Europe and the rest of the Western world, do not have the dollar. Nonetheless, they have followed a similar model using a carrot approach. The Automatic Exchange of Information, or AEOI is a reciprocity agreement whereby nation-states trade information on their citizens with each other. It was designed and put forward by the OECD, as they perceived that tax avoidance was becoming a problem and they were losing too much money through offshore entities transfer pricing schemes, and their citizens living abroad. Unlike FATCA, the AEOI went through a more prolonged acceptance process, with nation-states hiding behind their Westphalian exclusivity arrangements for many years before joining. The euro is not as 'in demand' as the US dollar and reciprocity being the key motivator to agreement implementation. However, as noted in previous chapters, standards between countries are not even. Information submitted to developed Western countries can be relatively assured to be kept private and on target for tax collection. Their institutions are robust with long histories. This is not so in other countries. The so-called "competent authority" (as the OECD puts it) in other, particularly developing, nation-states such as African and former USSR countries may not be so competent. There is real concern information given to these tax authorities in developing countries could be politically weaponized, given to fishing expeditions, or to outright extortion targeting of the less powerful for bribes and graft.

Both FATCA and the AEOI have similar prerogatives then: to shake the exclusivity of other nation-states in regard to people holding a passport from their country for needed revenue. The passport is the entire, and only mechanism for identification. While both have similar mandates they have different methods for compliance. FATCA uses threats, while AEOI uses carrots. They are also mutually exclusive. While FATCA and AEOI overlap, the US is not interested in reciprocity, rarely offers it, and does not subscribe to AEOI regimes. This hardcore stance is reflected in the universality of the dollar as the only game in town. Only with some very strategic partners, like the UK or Canada does the US begrudgingly allow reciprocity, which is more based on long-held tax treaties than on the advent of any FATCA benefice.

The lesson learned from both FATCA and the AEOI is that when it comes to wealth, which is the most highly prized denominator in the Westphalian system, sovereignty quickly gives way to practicality. This is an extremely interesting talking point, which will become even more clear in Chapter 10, Universal Enforcement. Pious declarations about the sanctity, national identity, and exclusivity of the nation-state are waived when push comes to shove with monetary matters. Consider how uber rich Switzerland was bullied to end its long storied banking secrecy in order to placate the US tax authorities. Being cut off from the US dollar would have devastated their prized banking sector. It also demonstrates further that certain high-cost Western nation-states cannot (and will not) structurally reform their systems. They must dig deeper into the barrel to keep their current political situations afloat. Resentment from citizens in a digitally empowered age will cynically continue to grow, as they watch more money go to finance military escapades, entitlements, and in promoting the welfare state, at their expense, without real changes. All the things that the digital age have laid bare and transparent. In essence Westphalia allows nation-states to become prisoners of their own systems, and use exclusivity to justify it to a point. This being the case, it will be hard to get national, let alone international cooperation on global public goods problems. If people don't trust their own government's motives, why would they trust another one?

China Taxation

As a postscript, China, the world's second largest economy has signed on to both FATCA and the AEOI, but hold these agreements at arm's length. China's trade also depends heavily on the dollar, but since China holds over $3 trillion plus dollars in reserves, and essentially loans money to the US by buying US Treasury bonds, the US government cannot bully China with FATCA as easily as it can with other dollar deficit countries. Turning over the records of foreigners residing in China is one thing, but committing the records of Chinese to foreign interests is another. China only recognizes Chinese citizenship, not dual. Nonetheless, dual citizenship still exists, especially within the Chinese diaspora abroad. China seeks to be a superpower, not just a regional power. In order to accomplish this, a robust tax system is in order, and like the others, China has a significant issue in restructuring its economy, both in terms of being export dependent and in dismantling its vast SOE network. However, the huge diasporas of overseas Chinese, with many still holding their Chinese passports, presents a target far too tempting to ignore. The problem that vexes China is subscribing to international conventions and sharing information. They have long sold their people on non-interference in others affairs, exclusivity, and the sanctity of sovereignty due to a long history of colonialism and subservience to foreign powers that they have vowed never to repeat. Sharing information is simply something China is not accustomed to doing, but as they evolve economically, they may be forced to. China's behavior may be a good litmus for determining the real motivations and standards of other nation-states in regard to public goods dilemmas. It seems that money must become the ultimate incentive for all concerned as the call to action.

Note

1. http://www.transparency.org/news/feature/corruption_perceptions_index_2016#table. Retrieved on August 2019.

CHAPTER 10

The Endgame: Enforcement and Acquiescence to a US-Led World Order?

Realpolitik

The purpose of this book is not to write merely an abstract or utopian academic treatise as to how things should be or could be in a world devoid of Westphalian constraints, but rather for suggestions in tackling global public goods problems on a *realpolitik* level, with productive results, and not an endless circular banter and hand wringing that respects the constructs of political boundaries at the expense of life on earth. We don't have time for that with such pressing global issues. In this sense, the climate change shill and media darling, Greta Thunberg, has a point. As we have stated unequivocally in Chapter 6, the world revolves around the US dollar. Despite the advent of the euro in 1999 and the Chinese yuan being added to the IMF's Special Drawing rights currencies in 2015, it is still the dollar that reigns supreme in all world transactions[1] (see Fig. 10.1). As such, any dollar transfers electronically or routed through the banking system are monitored by the US government, namely the US Treasury Department. Even someone, say, sending US dollars by wire from an account in New Zealand to next door Australia is logged and transacted in the US. Many books, essays, and seminars have been given about the preeminence of the dollar, accounting for nearly 65% of all world cross-border currency transactions, and its pending demise, due in part to a US national deficit of over $22 trillion and bloated military and social entitlement spending. Yet these predictions have never materialized. In short, the dollar is the all

© The Author(s) 2020
W. Hickey, *The Sovereignty Game*,
https://doi.org/10.1007/978-981-15-1888-1_10

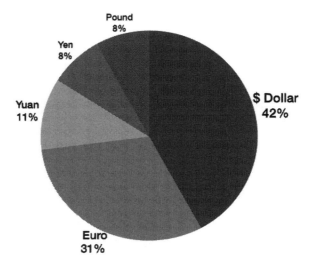

Fig. 10.1 IMF composition of Strategic Drawing Rights (SDRS) 2016 (*Source* IMF)

world currency. This also however presents a unique enforcement opportunity that may be lost in the scrum for abeyance to Westphalia. The US can enforce transactions through the dollar, it can also enforce laws via the dollar if used in fraudulent or illegal transactions. If we consider the likes of Seth Blatter (disgraced FIFA president) or Juan Guzman (Mexican cocaine cartels) or Huawei financial executive Meng Wanzhou, they were or are being prosecuted based on one mechanism, they routed dollars through the US banking system for a questionable activity, thus the intransigence happened on US soil, and in so doing breaking US laws, about corruption, drug trafficking, or trading with Iran. Even if they were far away from US soil, in Italy, Mexico, or China, when the said transactions occurred. Consider that if they had used any other currency, be it euros, Swiss francs, or Japanese yen, while still breaking US laws, cases would be much harder to prosecute them for abroad or to even extradite.

While in hindsight, it would be seemingly easy to switch to using other currencies, however, the counterparties to many of these transactions, the drug buyers, the sanctioned parts vendors, the illegal oil shippers, or bribe payers, who generally ply their trades specifically and holistically in dollars don't see it that way. They don't trust other currencies and don't understand them, their systems are based on dollars, so dollars become the default baseline. Other currencies such as yen, Singapore dollars or euros may also be fairly stable, but it is effectively a herd mentality with dollar. They know dollars, maybe euros, but anything else is suspect.

But this presents an interesting situation, if the US can enforce laws broadly based on the dollar and its use, is can then also enforce internationally agreed standards involving the dollar. This is in fact what the climate change crowd and many others want, and as we have stated throughout this book: universal enforcement. That being universal enforcement on those countries that break the climate accord laws, which are international in nature and thus meaningless in a Westphalian system. As we shall see in the key recommendation, a mechanism with carbon credits is with their pricing in dollars.

However, the problem with any universal enforcement is that it also flies dead against the Westphalian system of exclusivity that the political leaders and their elites hold so dearly. Or do they? Universal enforcement is particularly annoying to countries like China, or those countries with a long colonial past with Europe, such as in South America or Southeast Asia. They agree in substance with all the niceties of mitigating climate change, and cleaning up plastic waste, or global taxation sharing initiatives, but they reserve the right to do it on their terms, with many "exceptions" or on a differing standard. Exceptions mean leakage and loopholes, which puts a dent into the entire concept of robust enforcement.[2] Leakage and standards can also be politically manipulated, and Westphalia gives a wide berth for that to happen. This all means that universalism is null and void; and chaos theory reigns.

Carbon Credits and Pricing

Carbon credits are the desired CO_2 market mitigation mechanisms that underpin all the climate change accords from Kyoto to Copenhagen to Paris to the most recent COP25 in Madrid. As this is a political chapter, without going into rigorous technical details, carbon credits are essentially permissions to buy and sell carbon offsets for any industry or institution that pollutes or doesn't pollute against a baseline of allowable emissions for a city, country, or region. The key idea behind carbon credits is that efficient business and industry will be rewarded with credits to sell and inefficient, heavily polluting businesses will be penalized to buy credits with higher pollution costs used to fund renewable energy.[3] The goal of the credits then is to reduce industrial GHG (greenhouse gas) emissions nationally, and by extension, worldwide. For example, heavily polluting steel company (A) can buy credits off of green food company (B), which doesn't pollute as much or at all. A potential market is created. The emissions targets are set by the national government are divided and then allotted among all industries. Some industries receive more credits some less. How exactly the emissions are determined is up to each nation-state. Therein lies a major flaw in the accounting process. For example, emissions standards in Germany are no doubt more rigorous than in China, where heavily polluting industry is a main economic driver. Germany then could also set low amounts of credits available and China large amounts, meaning the credits would be costly in the EU, and cheap in Asia. In theory, an efficient and verifiable carbon credits market would allow the credits to traded globally, with the expectation of all inputs and outputs. Exchanging equal value for equal value. Without any verifiable way of actually tracking or auditing the emissions internationally (all countries claim that they have robust domestic emissions auditing and tracking) they can become political and subjective. At this point, carbon credits and offsets are largely a *voluntary* market. Meaning industry and institutions subscribe to them in good faith. Of course, this sets up all kinds of problems dealing with them effectively to reduce carbon, as the Westphalian system promotes exclusivity, all countries are on the "honor system". Simply put, that's not good enough. Any serious market must have a mechanism that will enforce the rules, uncompromised, either via a third party audit or by the blockchain (as discussed in Chapter 8). Otherwise, trust will be lost, and the market simply will not function or cease altogether to deliver on expectations. In retrospect, this has happened before when certain countries issued carbon credits that were then gamed by speculators,[4] and in short, the market collapsed.

Universal Enforcement Sought

The key issue then comes down to universal enforcement of the carbon credit market. And this is where the US dollar, with its ascription as the world's reserve (or actual) currency comes to the fore. It is noted that a true price for carbon has never been established. Proactive climate change countries like Germany seek a high carbon price ($100 per metric ton), to aid its green 'Energiewende' initiative whereas heavy fossil-fuel polluters like China or India seek a low carbon price (as low as ~$8 per ton) so heavy industry remains active. What is noted is that all proposed carbon credit prices are **always set in dollars**, never in euros, or yen, or yuan. This is similar to the oil business, where most key oil exporters set their prices in dollars also. US securities and exchange commission (SEC) enforcement is among the most diligent and respected in the world for guaranteeing the sanctity of contracts and due diligence in reporting. A hard example would be the US SEC form 20-F, which requires key information, detailed methods and timelines for foreign stock offerings in the US.[5] If a foreign company claims to have a process or procedure in place, and is listed on the US stock or CME commodities exchanges, the SEC may audit it, if discrepancies are found, at the least, corrections will be ordered, at the worst, fines and even jail time for executives.[6] This is the kind of enforcement the market and big investment banks like Morgan Stanley, Goldman Sachs, ultimately seek to back any carbon credit derivatives market. Universal enforcement, with strong accounting and audit mechanisms, backed up with real teeth to fine or imprison offenders. The assets they then deal in will be considered bona fide, with real authenticity and reporting under threat of punishment. While we are not suggesting the SEC form 20-F as the only document necessary for a nascent carbon credits market, it could provide a template model for an auditable compliance mechanism.

Simply, if using US dollars (that will definitely transit through the US system at some point) SEC enforcement for transparency/fairness could be considered in order, and with a large enough liquidity for developing any international carbon credits trading market. This would ensure proper registry, oversight, accounting methods, and forensic audit via the model of Sarbanes-Oxley (where CEOs go to jail if they signed a report that included deficiencies, false statements, perjury, or misrepresentations, whether they knew about it or not, ignorance is no longer an excuse) and including the use of any blockchain technology. China or EU countries can't do this of themselves, the former's markets are non-transparent and the latter's, not of the liquidity of the US. Australia and Japan are simply too small for universal compliance. Therefore, any patchwork to try to "mesh" a derivatives carbon trading market together under existing practices, without **US financial enforcement underpinning it, such as, the US SEC, or CME** will be fraught with loopholes that allow leakage, opt outs, and gaming by Westphalian actors. The big banks know this as do all the national leaders. In essence then, this is why Westphalia must be dismantled for any looming world catastrophe, otherwise, left alone, without universality, it becomes part of the problem, not the cure. Again, this type of enforcement could be extended to other issues, such as plastics pollution by placing a price on plastic, either single-use plastic or polyvinyl extrusions. For further introspect, we could also extend this to the bond market when Westphalian nations issue debt in dollars, not in their local currency. If they default, as Argentina did in 2001, and the bonds are liable in dollars, the courts with investor jurisdiction were in New York, not Buenos Aires. The point to all this is, when using the dollar for trade, enforcement mechanisms are rooted in US law, so why not carbon trading?

Could other exchanges also fill in? Possibly, but they are not using the dollar, so they lose one supercritical and key lever of enforcement. Another reason is that the markets know that the US SEC is possibly the most robust enforcer of financial rules worldwide, from insider trading, to misstatements, to ownership transparency. No other exchange requires this amount of high-level accountability. If a company wants to list internationally then, and seeks to avoid the US SEC, they list in London, which is less stringent, or Hong Kong, which is the least diligence required of all the major exchanges. This means that the less transparency and information available, the higher the risk for the investor. The markets are very good at determining value and risk. Carbon credits backed with market certainty would have real value.

We can also drive this further to get to international compliance then on a concerted level. Most of the world's countries have foreign exchange reserves in US dollar holdings. Some countries also have sovereign wealth funds,[6] compiled from their exports (usually from oil and gas, where much of the GHG emitted originated with their use) over the decades. These total holdings are also always reported in dollars. For example, Indonesia at the time of this writing holds $112 billion dollars in reserves, China holds $3.2 trillion, Saudi Arabia $500 billion. Norway holds nearly $1 trillion in its sovereign wealth funds alone. All countries heavily attached to fossil fuels and dollars. It is already noted that all electronic dollar transactions must pass through the US system, using either an ABA number or Society for Worldwide Interbank Financial Telecommunications (SWIFT) code. Extending this thinking then past carbon credits, if climate change is truly the humanity declared disaster that science says it is, then it would be easy to apply a credit check on other countries settling their transactions in dollars. At the least, through some type of verification mechanism, at the most, through perhaps a carbon tax on all dollar transfers. Of course, the writer is not oblivious **to the outrage this may cause among the Westphalian nation's sovereignty being violated**, but it would not be by political or military force, but rather by financial undertaking, with a foreign currency these countries have already wittingly used to underpin their own finances. However, we have already demonstrated that when it comes to dollar access, elites and leaders in their Westphalian nation-states will quickly waive aside domestic exclusivity concerns if their own wealth is threatened (Chapter 9, Taxation). If they didn't want to use dollars, they could opt out, but the world's economic behavior has told us otherwise in the most strongest terms. We are now cutting to the core of why Westphalia must go in the era of threats to humanity: it is an elite contrivance designed to uphold the status quo. Simply, countries use a world reserve currency from another country to underpin their own. If they are willing to give up a main tenet of domestic currency, namely, exclusivity for dollar usage, then other tenets can also follow.

THE US WILL BECOME THE NEXUS OF CLIMATE CHANGE MITIGATION

Despite President Donald Trump pulling out of the Paris Accords in 2017, the die is already caste, only the US with its dollar and financial enforcement mechanisms has the levers and enforcement ability to confront climate change head on with GHG emitters where it hurts the most: their pockets. This is not an endorsement to promote US hegemony or imperialism by any means, though it will no doubt be clearly interpreted that way by countries such as Russia and China and even the EU. They are not going to lower their Westphalian back door of exclusivity willingly, which they have fought hard to maintain over the decades and promote to gullible citizens. War is out of the question, all the big Westphalian states are nuclear armed with large standing armies. The only way to deal with climate change then on a completely enforceable level is through robust financial mechanisms people trust. Technological solutions that everyone will voluntarily embrace simply haven't born fruit, and well-wishing the problems disappear, is just that. Mechanisms that verify on an equal standard and hold accountable the emitters are necessary. Without that in place, we are merely having talks to have more talks or sing Kumbaya together. Meaningless and endless discussion with various Westphalian actors will not solve the CO_2 problem. It is already known what will solve it. Enforcement will. Countries in and of themselves under Westphalia will consistently default for ways out or to preserve their own economic advantages first. Dollar ascription changes this. Once in place, it forces an accountability they may not like or want, but will have to partake of for use of the dollar. Will they suddenly default to other currencies? History since Bretton-Woods in 1944 has shown the dollar has been king for 75 years, so there is no reason to believe they will now.

As an aside to all this, and at this current juncture of world politics, Trumpism, and Making America Great Again, and the US playing the role of world policeman, it could be a win: win: win. It gets other countries, in particular those who have contributed so much to climate change by burning fossil fuels, as payors into the system. It sets the US on track to earn a considerable amount of money by being the nexus for auditing and enforcing the carbon credit exchange system, and it puts the US back on the world stage for underpinning the global order. Far fetched? No. Obeyed by all? Yes.

We sum up this short but powerful chapter about why universal enforcement is needed and how it can possibly be accomplished with a Westphalian framework still intact, but its ability to obscure public goods problems dismantled: by money. Desperate times require desperate measures. Countries will kick and scream, but universal enforcement is needed to confront this issue, not platitudes. Nation-states will never let go of their sovereign fabric of Westphalia, as they simply have too much invested in it, and they can maintain that. National identity will always be an emotionally powerful construct, but a scientifically useless one. Westphalia must then be undermined by outside influences to be dismantled. In this case, dollar usage. Could it work? Definitely. Will the political blowback be huge? Definitely also. Will it mitigate GHG emissions at the 11th hour? Most definitely. The cure is worth the price at this late stage of climate change awareness, the world is depending on it, but not in the way the mainstream media, Westphalian politicians, science, and the financial industry has expected it, by playing neatly within the confines of Westphalia. This breaks that mold and pushes the envelope in a necessary direction.

NOTES

1. Desjardins, J. (2016) Demystifying the Chinese Yuan. http://money.visualcapitalist.com/demystifying-chinese-yuan/. Retrieved on June 29, 2018.
2. In 2007 the author had a minor research role for major Wall St. investment bank regarding feasibility of financing a carbon credit exchange. Throughout his work, he was surprised by two main things, first, the researchers

and traders were cocksure Hillary Clinton would be the 2008 Democratic nominee and would easily sweep to a presidential victory, ushering in an era of climate change activism namely enforcement. Second, the traders had no real concern about climate change, their primary goal was to get the SEC to develop an enforcement mechanism for carbon credits, similar to bonds and stocks, simply so they could trade them as bona fide sureties and make money. Without any universal enforcement, namely the US SEC, they couldn't be certain as to the value of what they were actually trading. Other countries, such as Japan and Australia had also issued carbon credits, but they were only as good as those nation-states borders, not universal.

3. Dowdey, Sarah. How Carbon Trading Works, August 27, 2007. HowStuffWorks.com. https://science.howstuffworks.com/environmental/green-science/carbon-trading.htm. Retrieved on February 21, 2019.
4. Sovacool, B. (2011) Four Problems with the Global Carbon Markets: A Critical Review. *Energy & Environment* 22 (6): 681–694.
5. The US SEC form 20-F is an extremely powerful tool used to enforce compliance from any foreign company seeking to list on the US stock exchange under threat of fines, perjury or company delisting. More can be read here: http://www.sec.gov/about/forms/form20-f.pdf.
6. Piotroski, J. D., and Srinivasan, S. (2008) Regulation and Bonding: The Sarbanes-Oxley Act and the Flow of International Listings. *Journal of Accounting Research* 46 (2): 383–425.
7. Hickey, W. (2014) Sovereign Wealth Fund Policy in the Information Age. *Harvard Kennedy School Review* 14: 94–98.

CHAPTER 11

More Sovereigns Not Less?

Is state sovereignty absolute as world interdependence grows?

UNDERCURRENTS

In a recent 2018 World Cup final featuring Croatia, a tiny nation-state that did not exist less than 30 years ago, shows us that Westphalia is still a powerful construct and national aspiration in today's age. However undercurrents such as blockchain, Social Media, Universal Basic Income, 5G telecom expansion, and of course climate change demonstrate the need for a unified, not unilateral or sovereign approach to issues, and that the nation-state tends to exacerbate public goods issues, not solve them. Territoriality however is a base or primordial instinct of humans and animals. Preserving differences with groups, clans, national identities becomes paramount, even though this trend has now been blurred by technology, migration and cross-border integration.

As this book has demonstrated, issues, trends, and problems are so amplified in today's data and media-driven world that the denominator of Westphalia has become outdated in its utility and usefulness. Of course that does not stop the reality of its political attainment, and in (and for) creating even more Westphalian states. It is of notice though that the final determining factor for legitimate Westphalian status is in

© The Author(s) 2020
W. Hickey, *The Sovereignty Game*,
https://doi.org/10.1007/978-981-15-1888-1_11

acceptance by the five large powers, or their blessing if one wills of the UN Security Council: the US, UK, France, Russia, and China. Without this unanimous acceptance, aspirational Westphalian states (Abkazia, Waz, Trans Dneper, Kosovo, Palestine, Kurdistan, etc.) are all left in a quasi-Westphalian limbo.

CONVERGENCE THEN OR DIVERGENCE?

The nation-state is not dead or dying. This book does not try to portray or insinuate that, though taken to its logical conclusion after reading this, it would seem very irrelevant. While nation-states have become more powerful the past 30 years, ethnic and religious groups inside those systems have also become more aggressive in seeking to establish their own states and territory inside those borders, such as the Iroquois nation in the US state of New York, or aborigines in NW Australia. We consider Uighers and so-called East Turkestan in western China as an example, or the very contentious Palestinian-Israel issue, or even the Rohingyas in Myanmar. Nonetheless, most national systems have far too much leakage across their borders than is ever publicized. The Western world may not clearly understand this issue that the media presents as universal. Scholars and activists such as Dambisa Moyo, Jeff Sachs, Nouriel Roubini, Joseph Stiglitz, Bill McKibben, and Chandra Nair all write piously about reforming the current "nation-state", so deeply engrossed in their circular thinking with old and disproven methods of industrialization, economics, and foreign reserves and seemingly oblivious to the interconnectedness of the digital age. Leakage means push and pull factors. People leaving or coming, smuggling, extra-territorial incursions, and extra-judicial decisions. That is the world we live in.

On June 4, 1989, Chinese tanks rolled into crush a student/worker uprising in Tiananmen Square in Beijing. While the causation was workers' rights and corruption, the response was to protect the stability and the status-quo elites of the Communist party behind it, let the masses be damned. The leaders of nation-states in developing countries are programmed to preempt any dissent, in particular anything dealing with ethnicity or culture, no matter how heavy-handed, consider Myanmar, Libya, Kazakhstan, Chile, Venezuela, Zimbabwe, etc., the list goes on and on.

Many also are simply placing far too much faith in multilateralism to solve today's global issues. After WWII, globalists believed that ongoing interaction and rebuild between nation-states would lead to a new order with supranational organizations like the UN, IMF, and World Bank growing in power, while the identity of the individual nation-state declined. This has not been the case, it has gone the opposite direction. The nation-state remains the preeminent entity behind today's global order. In essence, the West with globalization has become the antithesis of the developing world, which still clings to nationalism, dynasticism, and primordial ties. These ties can be especially strong in many South Asian and African cultures.

Nonetheless, nation-states are continually consolidating their power while at the same time, their religious and ethnic minorities are fighting for separation, autonomy, or outright independence (again, think Catalonia, Taiwan, Artsakh, or Papua in Indonesia). Only the biggest ethnic or religious groups inside national borders can push for autonomy or outright independence, such as conservative Muslims in Aceh province in Indonesia, or in Serbia, with Kosovo (still unrecognized by China and Russia). Smaller religious groups fall by the wayside, and get trampled by the majority, such as Rohingya Muslims in Bangladesh, Coptic Christians in Egypt, or Malaya Muslims in S. Thailand, all are historic minority religions in countries with a super-majority state religion. Also, undemocratic, authoritarian governments simply cannot be trusted to put forward minority rights, while conversely, some central governments do not even wield a controlling economic-political hand against some of their own wayward provinces or states, namely, these provinces and regions will set their own policies, if any, in abeyance of any compromised central government dictate.

Money and power go hand in hand, if they will keep governors (or warlords) in power there might be a fit with overall central government emissions goals, but recent history has taught this is wishful thinking. It is agreed that while none of these regions may add significantly to carbon, the precedent is set whereby they cannot be relied on to put emissions targets into action nationwide, ergo, systems leakage is only exacerbated. Here we consider some hard examples of more divergence of nation-states and aspirational ones.

Brexit—So much has been said about this already, the U.K., namely England and Wales, want out of the European Union, however it's two other large states, N. Ireland and Scotland, both voted to remain. This rift has forced a discussion concerning Scottish independence, and perhaps entering the EU by themselves. Currently, the Irish border issue is highlighting the total ridiculousness of Westphalia in a modern context.

They cant neatly solve the problem of Ireland being the only tangible border with UK and Europe. It simply confounds the Westphalian mindset of
borders and exclusivity. As of this writing, this issue regarding Brexit has
seemingly been settled with UK Prime Minister Boris Johnson's late 2019
election victory, but many details, especially border issues, are not easily
solved. EU politicians and UK parliamentarians worry and wring their
hands over the issue of having to reassert "borders" to control, assess,
and police. The handwringing is at core about reimposing a physical customs and immigration infrastructure in place to stop and check people
and goods going both ways, be it Calais-Dover or the Irish border. The
Irish on both sides (having a similar ethnicity, but two distinct political
groups) simply do not want a return to the old days which caused Ireland
so much grief politically. However, without infrastructure in place, goods
and people could flow freely across, thus jeopardizing and negating the
entire identity of the nation-state. In the twenty-first century though, one
may logically ask, "why are we still having discussions about fences and
gates"? Things can be tagged electronically with RFID chips, or placed on
the blockchain for provenance. In other words, the technology is there to
keep track of people and goods whether or not a physical border exists. It
is the policy (or lack of it, such as US state police not cooperating with US
Federal police in regard to illegal immigrants) that allows transgressions
to occur. Governments look backward, while the world looks forward.
We can also see with Brexit that it shows some states want out of the EU
convention, and others contemplate it more. The entire EU experiment
risks unravelling due to fiscal pressures; perhaps a predictor of any grand
nation-state union to confront climate change.

Catalan independence and Spain—The Catalan leader, Carles Puigde-
mont, voted unilaterally to leave Spain, by declaring Catalan independence, forcing a breach with the Spanish Federal Government in
Madrid. He later fled to Belgium, being charged with sedition in Spain.
Nonetheless, he continues to wage his fight for long aspired Catalan
independence, and has much of the population behind him, who dislike
Madrid's ruling hand. Madrid fears that if Catalan gains its independence, other states, like Galicia, could demand theirs. Further, Barcelona
in Catalan, represents a huge cash asset for all of Spain, letting it go to
independence would be a huge dent in Spanish coffers.

Bangkok and Southern Thailand—With the death in 2017 of the
socially and environmentally minded King Bhumibol, Thailand is poised
to lurch from crisis to crisis, with a military dictatorship seeking to

promise anything to Western countries, and their agreements, but not truly and legitimately able to enforce anything on a societal level. Islamic provinces in deep southern Thailand, which were long ago part of Malaya, seek their independence from the largely Buddhist state, or a Malaya reunification, the past many years, violence and discord are ongoing.

Egypt and the Sinai—Islamic extremists control much of the Sinai peninsula and cannot be reined in by Cairo's secular military dictatorship. They play off the animosity between Egypt and Israel to assert their control. The conflict is ongoing, but these groups largely run free.

Indonesia sans Bali/Java—Indonesia's economic clout and prosperity is all about Java and to some extent, the tourist resort of Bali. Outside those areas, central governance is weak with areas such as aboriginal Papua or Muslim Aceh seeking independence with continuing and simmering defiance. The central government has recently approved moving the capital from Jakarta to East Kalimantan, to better sector the economy, but they have never done a feasibility study nor have a clear idea of where the money will come from for this grandiose endeavor.

N. Burma and China—Much of northern Burma falls under Chinese sway, and is controlled by warlords. It is largely a "no-go" zone for the Burmese military, thus no central government presence can exist. China seeks to keep this and other areas as de facto 'buffer states' around it.

Syria/Iraq and Kurdistan—Nationalist Iraqi Kurds, heavily dependent on oil revenues thumb their noses at Bagdhad, not wishing to share oil revenues and setting their own political agenda in tandem with foreign oil companies. The US keeps a troop presence in Eastern Syria, allowing Kurds there to ignore Damascus' controls and create their own autonomous area. There is little, if any, central government control here, and formation of a new Kurdistan nation-state may be in its very early development.

East-Central India—Effectively a low-level communist insurgency has plagued these coal and iron ore producing areas of India for many years. Much of world press does not cover or understand the issues related to fighting over resources in poverty stricken areas. Unclear even if Modi's tough approach can integrate this area under strong federal control.

Libya—It is a political mess. US led Western coalition forces never had a governance plan for Libya past its deposed leader, Muammar Khadafi. Militias now run the oil-producing east, where Benghazi is, while the internationally recognized central government in Tripoli's control is weak.

Any international collaboration would be wishful thinking at best. Different factions control the country after Moammar Ghaddafi's overthrow. Nonetheless, so many factions are trying to reconsolidate a nation-state.

Sub-Saharan Africa—Many of these countries have weak central governance. Additionally blurred borders and constant war and foreign interference in these areas, either during war or for commodities showcase that the nation-state borders drawn by foreign powers, are still weak and in flux, for all the wrong reasons, not any shared commitment. Corruption in particular has been very rough on this part of Africa.

Palestine—The remains of the hastily concocted Sykes–Picot escapade of 1916 are considered with the current state of Palestine, uprooted by the big powers after WWII with the founding of the Israeli homeland. The entire issue has defined a long conflict between two incompatible religions, and defied an international solution for several generations. It is a sovereignty issue that cannot and will not probably ever be shared between opposing sides, and conflict continues.

What all the above demonstrate is that while social, data, and innovative trends are driving us further away from the nation-state construct, territoriality still reigns supreme in human nature, and thus people groups. They converge socially, but diverge nationally. Can the twain meet? Probably not. Nationalism is a powerful construct which tends to buoy the nation-state, despite the reality of the cross border issues that we have discussed at length throughout this book.

Nationalism Becomes More, Not Less

Globalization thus strengthens nationalism. Nationalism becomes an aspect of developing countries in particular clinging to primordial aspects of their culture, religion, dynasticism, or ethnicity against a context of a rapidly changing and very interdependent global word. If they do not fight to protect their identity, it will be lost. Nonetheless, the straight jacket of their own nation-states borders may also limit their own identities expression. The nation-state thus continues to remain the base denominator in the world we live in, and continues to prevail over internationalism, globalism, and most importantly, the solving of public goods problems. While theory should seemingly support a merging, or convergence, of identities, increased diversity, and shared cultures, especially with the technology and data on hand over time, the reality is quite different. The trend then is against working together to solve public goods issues collectively, as Westphalia allows a "hard border" in itself by preserving a nation-state's individual right of non-interference in its sovereignty. Nonetheless, public goods problems will continue to get worse not better over time. They do not wait for collective action, political niceties, or exclusivity to be debated forever. Governments may delay, but looming issues facing the planet will only continue to increase. This answer will not be found in platitudes about the 'sanctity of the nation-state' promoting faux diplomatic media releases, but ultimately in things that the key actors and their elites hold even more dear.

AFTERWORD TO THE SOVEREIGNTY GAME

Considering Hong Kong Independence in the Digital Age

The cover of this book has Hong Kong on it for a reason. It is an emblem of the sovereignty game. The writer has lived in both China and Hong Kong at different times over 25 years, including during the 1997 handover from the UK on a humid, rainy summer evening. The recent 2019 protests in Hong Kong have exposed intense generational conflict between those older people who identify themselves as Chinese, beholden to the political entity of the communist government in Beijing, and younger, technically adept and adroit, who identify themselves as Hong Kongers, or Hong Kong Chinese, who do not know Beijing or its communist party, except as negative history, from the Great Leap Forward, to the cultural revolution, and Tiananmen square. Their trust is lacking, and patriotism to any Communist identity non-existent.

This is similar to many young Taiwanese who consider their identity separate from mainland China. If one visits Hong Kong, or its neighbor, Macau, today, it is as if entering countries very separate from Mainland China. The thinking is different, the processes different, as are the languages. They are all de facto sovereign entities. The one country, two systems concept put in place by Chinese Communist premier leader Deng Xiaoping in a different century is outdated and flawed. Condominium (or co-sovereignty) has never successfully existed in the world, outside of a few islands and water areas split by bigger sovereign powers. In short

Hong Kong people have an identity problem caught between British colonialism and communist encroachment. However, this is not unprecedented, a way forward may still exist.

Singapore Independence

Singapore, a longstanding British commonwealth colony similar to Hong Kong, attained its independence from Malaysia in August 1965, under the misgivings, now revisionist history as "determinations", of Lee Kuan Yew. Lee did not want Singapore to leave the grand union with Malaysia, but was forced out due to economic imbalance, a Malaysian Cold War filter, and Malaysian/Chinese ethnic tension with Kuala Lumpur. No amount of revision today can change Lee's original lament over the then expulsion, "*I have believed in merger and the unity of the two territories*". The economic success of Singapore's to a "then go it alone" versus today's ASEANS financial hub has changed the conversation from regret to mountain apex in 50 years.

The Goa Rationale

Goa and India may be more of a proper comparison to China and Hong Kong with ongoing realpolitik. Goa was the crown jewel of Portugal'sAsian Empire for over 450 years, only later to be taken back by force from India in 1961. The Portuguese twofold argument with Goa, now consigned to the dustbin of history, or more plausibly, the fact that Portugal is a tiny country without overseas enforcement might, like the British with the Falkland Islands and Gibraltar, was that when Goa was established by them in the early sixteenth century it was with acquiescence by tribes in today's Gujarat state. In the seventeenth century, when Westphalia was established India did not exist as a coherent nation-state. Thus Goa and Portugal's claim, predated India as a political entity, though not a cultural one of course, and that Goa, since the 16th century was a longstanding metropolitan province of Portugal.

Similar reasoning today is also held with French Guiana and the Spanish enclave in North Africa of Ceuta and Mellila. That is, when these provinces or states were created by European colonial powers, there was no countervailing claim with an established nation-state on the other side. Nation-states as in today's definition, simply did not exist. Africa and South America were largely tribal areas, with vast swaths laying unclaimed.

Today, these areas are considered as integral parts of Europe, not merely colonial possessions, even though far away, as in the case of Guiana. Unfortunately, even though Goa claimed the same status as a metropolitan department of Portugal, India would have none of it and launched a military invasion in 1961. Goa had also been hollowed out by pro-Indian, anti-Portuguese forces for many years, and since tiny Portugal could not defend its far-flung province, it fell in three weeks.

The 1841 Treaty of Nanking and the Qing Dynasty

In 1841, the treaty of Nanking for Hong Kong island was between the Qing Dynasty and the British, in order to force open a foreign concession port. The Chinese Qing dynasty wanted it that way. If dynastic China was going to deal with imperialists, better to be in a port faraway from Peking. The founding of the modern Republic of China was not until January 1912 under Dr. Sun Yat-sen, and further, the founding of Communist China would not be until October 1949. Hong Kong predates both these events as a British trade colony in the mid-nineteenth century, bargained with the then Qing dynasty. No one would ever argue that Hong Kong is not culturally and ethnically Chinese, but is that identity ascription in itself enough to justify its assimilation into Communist China as just "another Chinese city" in 2047, when Hong Kong's status fully reverts fully back to the mainland? Namely, and similar to India with Goa, a country that did not exist as a nation-state later laid claim to, invaded, and absorbed another entity into its territory. Abstract theory? No. A reaffirmation of might makes right? Yes. Culturally relevant? Maybe.

The Bond Double Standard

Communist China today contends to usurp an agreement as its own that the British Empire made under a very different ruling body in 1841, when Communism did not exist. Karl Marx was still in graduate school in 1841, his manifesto would not yet be written for another seven years, in 1848. However, China is not consistent then in its handling of other agreements if this is the case with its sovereign absorption. We are talking specifically then about sovereign bonds issued during the Qing dynasty before 1911, later defaulted on, and which today's communist Chinese government (still) refuses to honor. In theory then, as the communist Chinese government in Beijing claims sovereignty over the whole of "China", it stands now as the inheritor of that debt issued pre-1911 also. In 1912, the Republic of China, China's first nation-state post its many dynasties, was founded under Sun Yat-sen. The Republic of China lasted until 1949, when it was ousted by the Communist Chinese and fled to Taiwan, where it is labeled as the Kuomingtan (KMT) party today.

Nonetheless, paying the bonds, about $1 trillion worth today, when considering inflation, currency translation, and interest, would strengthen Communist China's legitimacy on superseding both the Qing Dynasty and the Republic of China, in 1949. (Taiwan was recognized as the legitimate Chinese government until 1979, then unceremoniously kicked out of the UN.) Communist China's answer of course is that when the Communists took control of Beijing in 1949, the new government abolished all unequal treaties including canceling any foreign debts. The Peoples Republic of China stated officially that it does not have an obligation to pay back any outstanding debts after Chiang Kai-shek and the KMT fled to Taiwan in 1949 with a number of loans in hand.

This is not a frivolous argument made here. Consider that lesser countries, such as Argentina, have been forced to pay back bond issuance by the world markets long after governments have changed from socialist to military dictatorship to conservative. The markets (that is bond issues enforced through the US legal system in regard to any denominated in US dollars) demanded and doggedly pursued payouts, no matter who was in charge. Considering the amount of trade with China in dollars, and the fact that the Chinese yuan is pegged to the dollar, enforcing payment of these bonds is very possible. Could that be the price then offered to cement claims to Hong Kong? As a footnote, bonds issued under Tsarist Russia, which was overthrown by the Bolsheviks and Lenin in 1918, are still in limbo waiting to be repaid. The USSR ignored them as does Putin today, but the issue still smolders. Nonetheless, Russia unlike China, is not laying claim to a former British capitalist colony. The point is, China wants it both ways, they want to absorb Hong Kong, but ignore debt instruments generated from the same era.

Revisionist History Versus the Digital Age

Nation-states have had to consistently change the narrative, and why they did what they did, over time. All this worked fine while feeding a script to captive audiences inside tightly controlled or isolated borders. Whether it be communist, dynastic, feudal, or capitalist, leading and inoculating a local populace again "dangerous ideas" and "foreign influence" became a du jour saying.

Might makes right, such as with Goa in 1961 may have worked then, however instantaneous digital communication alongside social media forums with group discussion, has fractured this old playbook of forcing things from politics to economics to human rights to even culture. The digital age shows us that underpinning political power on culture, religion, or ethnicity is shaky ground., and that the "might makes right" argument of years ago only encourages more dissidence. By that consider many places with ongoing territorial strife: Syria, Kashmir, South Sudan. Allegiances, alliances, and other affinities now cross nation-state borders, and create different power groups that crystallize differing ideas. Consider the question "what is an American" as asked by minority right groups today brings on a multiplicity of confusing and angry discussion. Atomized information has empowered the individual and cannot be neatly and tightly contained by the nation-state. Simply, the cat of control cannot be put back into the bag.

Hong Kong is just the most recent example of this intergenerational and cultural clash. Information really is power, transcending the nation-states control legitimacy. In this case, a recent South China Post article by former Singapore diplomat Bilahari Kausikan noting that the entire protest movement is useless and will tightly be controlled by Beijing is wrong. This pessimistic author is stuck in another century and fails to understand (nor mention) that both the technical upheaval and generational issues give a false weighting to "national unity". Simply, it's the young people's future, not the old guards.

The realpolitik is that no one expects China to sever its tightfisted claim or control with Hong Kong as Kuala Lumpur did with Singapore in 1965. Chinese leader Xi Jinping and his Politburo legacy before him have made the reabsorption of Hong Kong into China a major tenet of their legitimacy. But all nationalist semantics aside, if the door can be left ajar, perhaps slightly, a logical discussion would be that perhaps China is better off with a prosperous and reliably independent Hong Kong on its doorstep as a proxy into China, similar to how it's been since Mainland China's economic liberalization in 1980. Its of note that some tiny countries in the EU, such as Andorra and San Marino are surrounded by giant neighbors, but are allowed to have their own governance functions and independence.

An independent and democratic Hong Kong could serve as an inter-locuter, as it's been doing, between the West and the Mainland, as opposed to economic juxtaposition to Beijing (i.e., 1965 Chinese major-ity Singapore and Muslim majority Kuala Lumpur is a pretext). Its inde-pendence could create an even stronger nation-state due to its strategic positioning between the worlds' two superpowers. We actually come full circle then, the entire reason Hong Kong was set up to begin with was as a liaison or a gateway between the British Empire and imperial, dynastic China. It has long since served that purpose, but could it use a rebooting in today's information-intensive digital era to amplify this rationale?

No doubt that this is a highly charged and contentious issue, where reason gives way to nationalist emotion, as Singapore also experienced in 1965 and Goa in 1961. The former gained independence unwittingly, the latter was denied independence and forcefully absorbed (despite any longstanding independence machinations) into India's political hegemony where no country called India, had ever existed before the Westphalian system of 1648. The Westphalian system of the seventeenth century effec-tively was about stripping the power of monarchies and religious orders and giving them to secular authorities. It was yesterday's solution to many acrimonious issues but has created today's problems in sovereignty claims.

Putting all nationalist histrionics aside (which may be an impossibil-ity), is that it may be of considerable economic and political benefit for China to give Hong Kong its independence, unlike what the British could not do, and not that it ever had any intention of doing. The digital age of AI, IoT, 5g, facial recognition, blockchain, Firefly, and Airdrops com-bined with attendant mass migration and crushing public goods problems (climate change, plastic waste, illegal immigration, overfishing..) has ren-dered so much of the original ideal of the "nation-state" and what it really stands for (exclusivity) and whom it most benefits (elites) moot.

Nonetheless, despite this truth, the trend worldwide has been for the divergence of more, not less, nation-states, such as Kosovo, South Sudan and the aspirations of such, Catalonia, Kashmir, and Artsakh, for exam-ple, accompanied by the populism as seen with Trump, Xi, and Putin in 'defending sovereignty' that goes with it. More rational arguments are needed, so who really gains by preventing Hong Kong independence or the independence of other would be nation-states?

BIBLIOGRAPHY

http://www.scmp.com/week-asia/opinion/article/3018003/harsh-truths-hong-kong-protests-will-not-achieve-anything. Retrieved on November 2019.

http://qz.com/1660460/hong-kong-protesters-use-airdrop-to-breach-chinas-firewall/. Retrieved on November 2019.

INDEX

Made in the USA
Middletown, DE
26 November 2022

16072407R00106